Praise for *Avoiding Anxiety in Autistic Adults*

'Framed around his golden equation, Dr Beardon's book highlights that anxiety for Autistic people exists not because we are predisposed to it, but as a very real and reasonable response to the negative consequences of the invalidating and often painful environments around us. Taking us through stages of when anxiety might be heightened, Dr Beardon validates Autistic experience; suggesting where Autistic people could take some control and focusing not on Autistic people as the ones who need to change, but instead on how those around us can and should change. This is a must read.'

Kieran Rose, The Autistic Advocate

'A vital addition to the shelves of autistic people and all of those who share our lives. So many excellent ideas, with insightful and important examples from the experiences of autistic people throughout. This book is easy to read, full of practical advice, and has led me to think deeply about autistic anxiety. From sensory and healthcare needs, diagnosis and employment, through to relationships and relaxation, there is something for everyone. Strongly recommend this positive, empowering book for all who are hoping to reduce anxiety and enable authentic thriving in autistic lives.'

Ann Memmott

'In his very readable book, Luke Beardon unpacks the many aspects of life that cause anxiety for autistic people, and suggests many ways in which the environment can – and should – be adapted to suit their needs. Covering crucial areas such as employment, healthcare and relationships, this book empowers autistic people and their loved ones to advocate for a better quality of life. As always, Luke's knowledge, passion and wealth of experience shine through every page.'

Heather Greatbatch

T0001765

Also by Dr Luke Beardon

Autism in Adults

Autism and Asperger Syndrome in Children: For Parents and Carers of the Newly Diagnosed

Avoiding Anxiety in Autistic Children: A Guide for Autistic Wellbeing

Avoiding Anxiety in Autistic Adults

I have been working in the field of autism for decades, in capacities ranging from practitioner to researcher to trainer to lecturer. My work has involved helping local authorities to develop services and good practice, coordinating and developing services and training for the National Autistic Society (NAS) and being part of a research team at Nottingham University. I have also spoken at a number of national and international conferences on a variety of autism-related topics.

Presently I am a senior lecturer in autism at Sheffield Hallam University. I am the course leader for the postgraduate certificate in autism and Asperger syndrome, run in collaboration with the NAS, and supervise several students at doctoral level, many of whom are autistic. I am very proud that several of my autistic (ex) students have completed their doctorates successfully. I also continue to be involved in research in a wide range of autism-related areas.

In 2011, I was awarded the Inspirational Teacher Award, in 2012 the Inspirational Research Supervisor Award and, in 2018, my third Inspirational Award. In recognition, my university presented me with the Sheffield Hallam Vice-Chancellor Award. In 2015, I was a finalist for the prestigious NAS's Lifetime Achievement Award for a Professional. In 2016, I was the winner of the NAS's Autism Professionals Award for Achievement by an Individual Educational Professional. In that same year I was also nominated and reached the finals for the Autism Hero Awards in two categories – Lifetime Achievement and Individual Professional – and won both categories.

Occasionally, I have made media appearances, including on the BBC and Radio 4, and featured in articles that have been published in *The Guardian*, *The Independent* and *The Times*. In the award-winning *Aukids* magazine, in its list of the top ten all-time favourite autism blogs, mine reached the number two spot.

In other writing, I co-wrote the ASPECT consultancy report (2007) – the largest consultation ever undertaken with adults with Asperger syndrome until that time. I have co-edited five books on autism and Asperger syndrome, I wrote *Autism and Asperger Syndrome in Adulthood* (2016), *Autism and Asperger Syndrome in Children* (2019) and *Avoiding Anxiety in Autistic Children* (2020) and have written various other pieces published in journals and books.

Overcoming Common Problems

Avoiding Anxiety in Autistic Adults

A Guide to Autistic Wellbeing

DR LUKE BEARDON

sheldon PRESS

First published in Great Britain by Sheldon Press in 2021
An imprint of John Murray Press
A division of Hodder & Stoughton Ltd,
An Hachette UK company

4

A CIP catalogue record for this title is available from the British Library

Trade Paperback ISBN 9781529394740
eBook ISBN 9781529394757

Typeset by KnowledgeWorks Global Ltd.

Printed and bound in Great Britain by Clays Ltd, Elcograf S.p.A.

John Murray Press policy is to use papers that are natural, renewable and
recyclable products and made from wood grown in sustainable forests. The
logging and manufacturing processes are expected to conform to the environmental regulations of the country of origin.

John Murray Press
Carmelite House
50 Victoria Embankment
London EC4Y 0DZ

Nicholas Brealey Publishing
Hachette Book Group
Market Place, Center 53, State Street
Boston, MA 02109, USA

www.sheldonpress.co.uk

To Professor Alan Beardon; many years ago as your youngest child I was included in a dedication in one of your books; I am honoured to be able to return the sentiment, honoured to be your son, and honoured to have been exposed to the incredible wisdom that you have imparted over the years. You are an extraordinary man.

Contents

Acknowledgements

To the autistic tribe who allow me into their lives, unselfishly, empathically, with kindness and generosity, sharing their experiences, adding to my understanding, and, I hope, making me a better human.

And to my wife, Kate, and boys, Fionn, and Guy; as always, without you, I am nothing. I can face all the anxiety in the world knowing you are by my side.

1

Autistic anxiety

Anxiety. At best it makes for a pretty miserable day. At worst – it kills. Make no mistake – this is no hyperbole, no exaggeration, no fabrication – the kind of ongoing, perpetuating, seemingly never-ending, dark, intense, consuming anxiety that can pervade the lives of autistic adults has the capacity to cripple a person's wellbeing and disastrously impact on mental and physical health. The long-term impact of ongoing anxiety cannot be underestimated. To wake up with the knowledge that you are anxious, and to go to bed knowing that the same anxiety will stave off sleep or intrude on dreams, with no certainty as to when the cycle will ever end, is to lead a desolate and distressing existence. If you are an autistic adult reading this who does not recognize yourself in these opening words – fantastic. I hope that you continue in an anxiety-free world. If you are an autistic adult who recognizes, at least in part, some of these words – then I reach out to you through this book in the hope that it might, in some way, help alleviate aspects of your anxiety. If you are a person reading this to better understand autistic anxiety, possibly (hopefully) to better understand someone you care about and/or support them, then please take this introduction seriously.

Anxiety is the state that one might find one's self in for any number of reasons. Sometimes it's a myriad of combined factors that lead to anxiety; sometimes it can be a very specific trigger that is identifiable. Whatever the reason, anxiety cannot ever be underestimated in terms of the devastating impact that it can have on a human – which is why it needs to be taken so seriously. Fear, frustration, confusion, interaction, the sensory environment, the unknown – any one of these (and the list could be extended multiple times) can lead to acute anxiety – it's rarely an easy area to circumnavigate and understand – if it was, then it wouldn't be a problem. And it really is a huge problem. There are

1

statistics relating to autistic anxiety that demonstrate that you are far more likely to be anxious than the PNT – and for many adults anxiety can be a diagnosable pathological psychiatric state – and yet I wonder if those statistics are even close to the reality. One of the issues that so many of you face is that having been in a constant state of anxiety for much or even all of your life, it becomes such a norm that you don't necessarily consider that life could be any different. I've known plenty of adults who don't know that they are in a more anxious state than the rest of the population because it has never occurred to them. We could be living in a world where there are far more anxious autistic adults than research has identified – not least because many of those adults remain unidentified anyway.

Before I continue, I shall explain my terms. *I* – means *me*; my views have developed through many years of being allowed to share the lives of autistic people. I also happen to live a pretty autism-focused life, as autism is my job and has been (on and off) since I first knowingly came across autism as a volunteer in a special school, aged 14. I would consider myself a 'practice-based' academic for want of a better phrase. I am absolutely not an autism expert – no one is. Some people will be experts in a particular area of autism – a particular age group, a particular person (you may well be an expert in your own autistic self) – but as the numbers of autistic people are so vast, and the range of how autism impacts on each individual at any one time is infinite, my belief is that to claim expertise in a population that is so prolific would be an indication that, in reality, the claimant is far from being an expert simply by claiming to be one. However, I have been fortunate enough to share the lives of many autistic people over many years – directly and indirectly – and each day that goes by adds just a little more to my understanding.

Most books written about autistic people write 'about' you. I do not intend to do that. You are the centre of this narrative, *you* being the autistic person. Many of you will have been 'othered' to the point of it being the norm – which in itself can be a cause of anxiety. Yes, being autistic by definition is to be different to the majority – but it is by no means to be lesser, which is often how the autism narrative is presented. I do not subscribe to this notion. So – *you* means the autistic reader. I will also refer to autistic adults in the third person – this is more to assist with narrative flow than anything else; however, it is also a necessity when including examples of real life.

Note – I use the term 'autistic' as opposed to 'with autism'. As with 'neurodiversity', there is much debate as to which should be the preferred term. History can clearly demonstrate movement in this regard, which is both refreshing and somewhat depressing simultaneously. It used to be the case that there was a very clear dictate that using the identity-first term 'autistic' as opposed to the person-first term 'with autism' was not the done thing; the insinuation being that being referred to as autistic was a negative. When I first started my academic journey this 'rule' was extremely clear. However, in recent years there is plenty of evidence that autistic adults far prefer the identity-first 'autistic' to ascribe to their autistic self. Research papers as well as the plethora of Twitter polls (I read one last week with over 6,000 responses – 91 per cent choosing identity-first language) and blogs of autistic adults show a very clear preference. This is extremely refreshing – the fact that many authors are actually listening to the autistic population and changing their language use is hugely encouraging; what is less encouraging is the ongoing narrative that does not take these preferences into account! It should also be noted that while the majority of individuals prefer identity-first, there is a significant minority who are happy with either term, or specifically align with person-first language.

Many authors will use terms such as 'neurotypical' and 'neurodiverse'; these are perhaps more complex than one might think – some will refer to non-neurotypical individuals, for example, as 'neurodiverse' when 'neurodivergent' is the accurate term – after all, one individual cannot be of multiple neurologies. A population is, of course, neurodiverse; an individual is not. This may sound pedantic, however it is a good illustration as to the sometimes subtle ableist language that perpetuates literature relating to autism that leads to anxiety. If one is constantly exposed to language of deficit and comparison, then it is likely that this will have a negative effect on one's mindset. The idea that there is one 'right' way of being within neurological function, and to differ from that 'norm' is somehow to be lesser, is a notion that needs to be challenged in the strongest terms within the autism world. The reality is that it is a biological fact that the entire human race is neurodiverse – but there are groups of individuals within that diversity that can be seen and understood within different paradigms – neurodivergent and autistic being two of those groups (all autistic individuals by definition will be neuro-divergent – not all neurodivergent individuals will be autistic). My preference, rather than neurotypical, based on an email sent to me by an autistic adult who I was lucky enough to know, is 'predom-inant neurotype' – abbreviated to PNT. So – to be clear – the PNT by statistical definition would not be autistic. This is how I will refer to the population who are not autistic – while absolutely accepting that there will be wonderful pockets of humanity whereby the PNT is actually autistic. I am also acknowledging that within the PNT population there will also be neurodivergent individuals who are also not autistic; however, as this book is about autistic anxiety and not, specifically, the neurodiversity paradigm or movement I shall leave those debates at that. I apologize for being so binary about this, and absolutely understand and accept that the neurodiversity of the human race is far more complex than this scant section indicates. The other aspect that might be useful to include here is that those who are not autistic but who experience severe levels of anxiety (for whatever reason) might also find some of this narrative of benefit.

So – back to my opening section – you will notice that I have included the term 'autistic anxiety'. I should be absolutely clear, here – there is no 'ownership' over anxiety. It is not the sole domain of the autistic population by any stretch of the imagi-nation – after all, anyone can be anxious – and some of the PNT will at times be just as anxious as any autistic person. But I genuinely believe that there is *in the main* a qualitative difference between your way of experiencing anxiety and the anxiety experi-enced by the PNT. This will not always be the case – but for most of the PNT compared to most of you there will be less overall ongoing anxiety, less frequency, less duration, less intensity, and fewer days during which anxiety is experienced. The reason for this, in a sense, is somewhat simple – but is a notion that can go an awful long way in ascertaining what we need to do about autistic anxiety; apologies for repeating myself, as I have written and spoken about this several times before – but it comes back to what I refer to as the golden equation:

$$\text{Autism} + \text{Environment} = \text{Outcome}$$

What this means is that being autistic in and of itself means nothing aside from the fact that you are autistic. It literally cannot go any further than that in relation to outcome. All of those statistics around what being autistic means are up for debate until the statistic is 100 per cent – i.e. when a specific outcome for all autistic individuals is identical. There is very little that can fall into this category! If you try to complete the sentence 'All autistic people will definitively . . .' you will soon discover that there are very few endings that can be applied that are relevant to all autistic adults. In fact – and while I don't want to contradict the purpose of this book – it is crystal clear that being autistic is not the same as being anxious – otherwise all autistic people would, presumably, be anxious, all of the time – which is absolutely not true. It would be just as valid to acknowledge that there are some autistic people who very rarely experience anxiety. However, I still maintain that being autistic in an environment that is unsuited to you, will lead to far greater risks of high anxiety. The problem that so many of you will know about is that the environment is so often unsuited – in which case the probability is that there is a higher risk of anxiety. I could argue (in fact I do argue) that there is a direct correlative link between the levels of environmental suitability and the levels of anxiety that are likely to be experienced. Simply, the more suitable the environment, the less the likelihood that you will be anxious.

So – what do I mean by environment? Categorizing loosely, there are three main components that impact on the environment within the above equation – these are the three main areas, I am by no means suggesting that they are exclusive. So the three main components are:

1 People
2 Physical environment
3 Systems – e.g. policy, strategy, legislation

If we get all of the above 'right' – in terms of reflecting your individual need – then the chances are your anxiety will take a back seat. Unfortunately, as you will no doubt be aware, these ideal circumstances are few and far between. The main point I am making here is that it is the environment that is the biggest influencer over your anxiety – not you. There may be things that you as an individual might be able to do to impact on your anxiety – but most of the time your anxiety will stem from the environment, not from within yourself, so the focus should be on changing whatever the cause is within the environment, rather than the focus purely being on you.

This book is not intended, therefore, to be a self-help manual for you – that would be beyond patronizing at best. It does, however, seek to identify what might potentially be causing your anxiety in order for something to be done about it. In fact, while this book is directly written to you, it could be that, if it is to be of benefit to you, it should be read by others around you who may have influence over your environment.

When I came up with the idea for this book, I was hoping for it to be a guide to some of the pitfalls that you might encounter through adulthood – and possible ways to avoid them. I hope that there will still be some elements of this within the chapters – but actually, so many of the anxiety-inducing experiences that you will have faced are so dependent on others that much of this book has been taken over by suggestions for how others might change their practice in order for you to lead a stress-free adulthood. While there are some aspects of life that you have total control of, and some aspects that you might have partial control over, there are still many areas that are beyond your control. Therefore it is vital that the general population understands what many of the issues are, and is educated to respond accordingly. It should not 'simply' be down to you to work out what the solutions are, and to implement them.

The way in which I have gone about writing this book is to identify some key areas that are likely to be a part of your life, and to subsequently indicate what aspects of those could cause anxiety. I will also make suggestions as to what might change in order to reduce some of those effects. These suggestions are not legally binding, but they do have the legislation of The Equality Act in mind. The Equality Act recognizes autism as a disability and therefore there is a legal duty to take the following types of discrimination into account:

Direct discrimination is when an institution acts less favourably towards you as a result of you being autistic. An example of this might be an employer who decides that you should not be shortlisted for a job because you are autistic.

Indirect discrimination is when you are disadvantaged because the policy (or similar) is applied in the same way, not taking your autism into account. An example of this might be that you are forced into sharing the same sensory experience that could have been avoided, which puts you at a disadvantage.

Discrimination arising out of a disability is when you are treated unfavourably as a result of something specific to how autism impacts on you. An example might be that you need to have time to process information following a colleague's presentation prior to joining the Q&A session but are not given the time to do so.

Reasonable adjustments are to be put in place to ensure that you are not put at a substantial disadvantage as a result of being autistic compared to others. I will be giving examples of what might be considered reasonable adjustments throughout the rest of the book; there is no clear definition as to what a reasonable adjustment actually is, though there are guidelines. This is a positive and a negative – positive in that it recognizes just how individual some of your adjustments need to be, but problematic as there are grey areas around what needs to be lawfully provided/changed and what doesn't. The examples I will give take the following into account, as per the guidelines: changing the way things are done, changing the physical environment, and the provision of additional aids and/or services. There is not an unlimited resource for those under the Act to provide adjustments, so there are other considerations that need to be taken into account, for example, the information from Citizen's Advice is as follows:

Adjustments only have to be made if it's **reasonable** to do so. What's a reasonable thing to ask for depends on things like:

- your disability;
- how practicable the changes are;
- if the change you ask for would overcome the disadvantage you and other disabled people experience;
- the size of the organization;
- how much money and resources are available;
- the cost of making the changes;
- if any changes have already been made.

I will endeavour to remain within these guidelines throughout the book – but do take note that I am not a solicitor!

The rationale behind including what might be considered reasonable adjustments in a book on autism and anxiety is that I fully believe that a lot of the anxiety that is experienced by you could be avoided if The Equality Act was adhered to on an individual basis, with an understanding of individual autistic need. Consider the following scenarios as examples of reasonable adjustments that made a massive difference to the individual:

Alan is an academically stand-out student who has completed his PhD thesis and is ready to prepare for his Viva Voce. The Viva has been allocated a room by the university's room booking team and, despite Alan being known to the university as being autistic, the room has bright fluorescent lights, two clocks, both of which have audible ticks, and is adjacent to the cleaning cupboard which has strong smelling disinfectant. Alan has sensory sensitivities as a result of being autistic that include a strong aversion to fluorescent lights which give him a migraine, auditory sensitivity which means he hears background noise at the same level as any other noises in the vicinity, and olfactory sensitivity which means that if there are strong smells nearby he cannot process language at the same speed as within a more smell-neutral environment.

This is not a particularly unimaginable scenario – and many PNT, who may not understand autism very well, might not understand just how genuinely disadvantaged by the environment Alan actually is. The reality, however, is that Alan, despite years of hard graft, is in danger of failing his Viva due to adjustments not being made. This is the harsh reality of autistic life for so many people – the PNT do not seem to understand the very real and very devastating impacts of not taking autism and the environment seriously. In Alan's case, as it happened his supervisor was very familiar with Alan's needs, and understood his requirements. One of those requirements that the supervisor had taken upon himself was to show Alan around the room several days prior to the Viva, as this would help reduce the anxiety of Alan not being able to visualize the room prior to entering it. As a result of visiting the room Alan and his supervisor were able to identify the pitfalls of the room allocation; the very simple solution that cost no money was to get an alternative room allocated; Alan passed the Viva with no problem at all.

This example illustrates a number of things that might cause anxiety – along with what can be done about them, with a clear way forward that is massively impactful on the individual. And yet I hear of so many students for whom such adjustments are summarily ignored – and who knows what long-term damage is being done to those individuals?

I am fully of the belief that language and concepts can be massively influential on mental wellbeing. For example, I know that some autistic adults will not discuss autism with the PNT simply because the level of ignorance and harmful myths that surround autism within Western society are too difficult for them to be exposed to (see Chapter 5 for more on disclosure). I'm sure that many of you will be well aware of these kinds of scenarios, so the next few examples/myths are more intended for the reader who is less likely to have been exposed to harmful narrative.

Some people, on hearing that you are autistic, will respond with an assertion that it must mean that you are either very good at something ('So that makes you a genius at [insert nonsense here] doesn't it?!') or else very poor at something ('That means you can't have any friends?' – or similar). What is problematic isn't quite so much related to the inanity of the assertions themselves, though these are harmful in their own right, but to the very fact that people make the extraordinary assumption that they can judge you as a human being based on aspects of your autism that bear no relation to you.

I suggest that a widespread reasonable adjustment that could so easily be picked up is a blanket 'never assume anything about a person solely based on their identification of autism' – see, how simple would that be? And what a difference it could make! Straightaway, if everyone were to buy into this suggestion, disclosure would not risk opening you up to a hurtful narrative; it would increase the chances of the other person making enquiries as to what impact autism has that are specific to you – which is a better way to engage you compared to making assumptions. Throughout the text I will highlight my favourite adjustments in the hope that one day they can be incorporated into The Autism Act (these are also listed together in the Appendix). The first on the list is:

> When someone discloses their autism to you, respond by asking what autism means to them as an individual, rather than making any assumptions based on the autism label itself.

Actually, while I am in mind of reasonable adjustments, I shall quickly follow with my second, and it's a potential game-changer:

> When you are engaging with an autistic person, always ask yourself the question: 'Am I doing everything reasonable in my power to identify anxiety and subsequently doing everything I can to reduce or eliminate it?'

Imagine if this was a dictate that all people adhered to all of the time – the impact it could have, often at no financial cost, is huge. I genuinely believe that there is a lot to be said for promoting the notion that ignoring the fact that *autism + environment = outcome* could, in certain circumstances, be unlawful in and of itself. If we can accept that being highly anxious leads to a deterioration of functioning – which it does – then surely this could put you at a significant disadvantage. If you are at a significant disadvantage as a result of your disability (in legal terms) – and autism is one component of the above equation, so it stands to reason that it is covered under The Equality Act – then not making reasonable adjustments to reduce anxiety could be seen as unlawful. If it is reasonable, for example, to expect those around you to be consciously aware of what might cause you anxiety – and subsequently to avoid those triggers – then it would be unlawful for those people *not* to make those adjustments. In many situations it really is as simple as that. So one could even argue that, if we as a society have an understanding that environmental factors are likely to increase anxiety for you, then by not making a reasonable effort to ascertain what those factors are could constitute unlawful action. Consider the following linear progression:

1 Do I understand that environmental factors might cause anxiety for an autistic person?
2 Do I understand that those environmental factors include me as an individual?
3 Have I made a reasonable effort to find out how my actions (or inactions) might increase anxiety for this autistic person?

If the answer to 1 and 2 are a 'yes' and the answer to 3 is a 'no' – could this mean that I am acting unlawfully? What this means is that knowledge is power – as a society it is imperative that there is a better understanding of the lawful ramifications for not taking autistic anxiety seriously. Teaching the pretty simple concepts already outlined in this chapter could be a major way forward in the reduction of your anxiety – at least that's the hope. As noted, I am not legally trained – but my lay person's way of understanding how I could reduce risk of acting inequitably is by asking the following questions:

1 Is this autistic person at a significant disadvantage within her current situation, in which I have some influence, as a result at least in part of being autistic?
2 If so, what might I reasonably be expected to do in terms of action to redress that inequality?
3 Have I made every reasonable effort to act in that manner?

If the answers are 'yes' for 1 and 'no' for 3 then I need to consider whether I am acting unlawfully. Here are some very simple examples for consideration – I am not claiming that they are legal examples, but it is worth thinking about them nonetheless.

Beatrice is an autistic student within Higher Education. She has declared being autistic to the university and made it clear that she has processing difficulties with visual materials, such as presentations. If she doesn't have access to such material in plenty of time in advance, her anxiety increases and makes the situation even worse. The lecturer decides that her request to make the presentations he uses available a week prior to delivery is too much to ask.

In this example, I would suggest that the lecturer is likely to be acting unlawfully. He knows about Beatrice being autistic, and that her processing of his material requires longer compared to her PNT peers. It would appear reasonable to expect him to allow his presentations to be available a week prior to delivering them, and by not doing so could be putting Beatrice at a substantial disadvantage.

Carl is an excellent employee who is very effective at his job. However, he steadfastly refuses to join in team meetings in the same vicinity as his colleagues, insisting that he gets far too anxious and that accessing those meetings remotely is just as effective. His anxiety is such that he cannot effectively input into the meetings, whereas in the safety of his own home he would be relaxed enough to be a productive member of the meeting. His employer is resistant to 'allowing' Carl to do so, saying that, 'It is usual practice for everyone to be in the same room, and it would seem odd if you were not physically present.'

Again, there could be an argument here that the employer is acting unlawfully. Is Carl at a significant disadvantage? Yes. Would it be reasonable to give Carl the option of being present in a remote capacity rather than physically present? If the answer to this question is 'yes' then surely he should be allowed that option.

Daphne finds supermarkets absolutely overwhelming from a sensory perspective, which means she can only be within one for brief periods of time otherwise she suffers from intense migraines. She makes enquiries about getting placed on the priority list for home delivery slots but the supermarket refuses, suggesting that the priority slots are there for people who cannot access the store for physical reasons.

Once again, one could put forward the case that this is unlawful. Just because Daphne is physically able to access the store does not mean that it would not put her at a substantial disadvantage by having to do so; it would seem reasonable to put Daphne on the priority list for home delivery in this instance.

Back to language and concepts – the current parlance around autism is almost entirely negative and medical-model based (i.e. based on a deficit model that there is something 'wrong' with you that needs fixing). I absolutely disagree with this model. I am well aware of the struggles that you face, and well aware that for some, being autistic is something that they would prefer to change – but I maintain that it is the combination of you as an autistic person and the problematic environment that causes the difficulty, not being autistic per se. Therefore, if one wants to change the outcome, it should be the environment that is under investigation more frequently than you. I must reiterate – after all, this book is written about your anxiety – I am not diminishing the very real and very negative impact that being autistic in many environments can have on you – but I also fervently believe that making the changes to those environments will go a very long way towards creating a wholly positive experience. Therefore, I reject the notions of disorder, deficit and impairment that litter the autism narrative. I will come back to this when exploring the whole notion of diagnosis, but in the meantime I wish to express my opinion that the notion that autistic people are somehow lesser is a pure myth. Just because my goose doesn't quack does not make it an impaired duck. Just because my duck can't hiss does not make it a goose with a deficit. I am not suggesting that autistics and PNT are different species, by the way – the same analogy could be applied in all sorts of ways, but the concept remains the same – difference does not equate automatically to impairment.

I have written elsewhere about common myths (please see the Further reading page), so I will not explore this too much further here, but there are some additional ones that are noteworthy in addition to those identified above:

1   Autistic women do not exist
2   Autism is related to intellectual ability

The former should speak for itself – and yet it is still clear that there are many who believe that women are less likely to be autistic, as opposed to less likely to be identified – there is a huge difference between the two. I do not believe for one moment that women are any less likely to be autistic compared to men, but I absolutely understand that women have a much harder time in being formally recognized as autistic within the same comparison. This brings its own set of frustrations and anxiety, as can be imagined.

In terms of intelligence – simply, being autistic has nothing to do with intelligence; there is the same range of intellectual ability within the autistic population (i.e. from those who may have additional learning disabilities through to highly intellectually able adults) as there is within the PNT population.

2

Experiencing anxiety

I identified the notion of 'autistic anxiety' in Chapter 1 and, while making the point that anxiety is not the sole domain of the autistic population, there does seem to be differing experiences for many autistic adults in comparison to many of the PNT. This must be made absolutely crystal clear – some autistic adults will be pretty much anxiety free, and some of the PNT will suffer from anxiety just as much as any autistic person – however, there is still evidence that supports the concept that you are more likely to suffer from anxiety, which may well manifest in a different way, compared to others; this is why I believe that the term 'autistic anxiety' is a valid one.

Irrespective of statistical data, if you suffer from autistic anxiety then that is enough reason for me to be writing about it. I am very well acquainted with enough adults to recognize that anxiety can be experienced in intense fashions, with a hideous degree of frequency, and over prolonged periods of time. This is not the norm for the majority of the PNT. So – those three components of intensity, frequency and duration (see below for more on these) are important to recognize for yourself or anyone interested in identifying the impact of anxiety in adulthood. This might sound as if it's obvious – but it isn't. Many of you who are anxious may not realize just how different your lived experiences are compared to the majority of the PNT – if it is so common to feel the way that you do it might be that you assume it is the same for everyone else. Another reason that may impact on how aware you are of your own emotional states, including anxiety, is alexithymia. This refers to one's ability to recognize and label emotional states, both in one's self and in others. Autistic individuals may be more likely to be impacted by alexithymia than the PNT, so it is well worth taking the time to look into it if you feel that it relates to you. One of the things that I advocate for is support in understanding of emotional states – the better acquainted you are with how you actually feel, the better your chances of doing something about it. The three components of anxiety you need to learn to recognize are:

- The **intensity** of the feeling of anxiety – this could be regarded as the peak, the point at which you feel the very worst kind of anxiety over a period of time. Many of the PNT will only experience intense anxiety extremely infrequently – so if you suffer from intense anxiety (the kind that leads to a fight or flight response, or meltdown, or shutdown) then it is important for it to be recognized.
- The **frequency** of feeling anxious is also worth identifying. Are you anxious on a daily basis? How many times per week do you feel anxious? By 'feeling anxious' I mean those moments in which you are consciously aware that you are feeling anxious – as above, many of the PNT will only be consciously anxious on an infrequent basis.
- The **duration** is how long each episode of anxiety lasts for. My belief is that for many of you each episode of anxiety is likely to last much longer than anxiety experienced by many others. It all takes its toll.

Taking these three aspects of anxiety, then, creates its own three-dimensional model that could be useful in identifying your own experiences. There is no 'one size fits all' when it comes to autistic anxiety, but these three facets are worth taking into consideration. Ask yourself which is the biggest issue – the intensity, frequency or duration of your anxiety? Is it a combination that leads to a worst-case scenario?

In relation to the third facet, duration, it is notable that many of you might exist in a *constant* state of anxiety; this might be considered low-level – but some of you may experience higher levels of anxiety still as a constant presence. As noted above, this is not an emotional state for most people, and most certainly must not be accepted or ignored. To live with constant anxiety is a misery that no one should have to endure. One of the very real issues that ongoing anxiety can have, or a combination of the above facets of anxiety, is the risk of developing complex post-traumatic stress.

I am convinced that this is still not nearly as recognized as a life risk factor for autistic adults as it should be. It might be that a whole childhood of ongoing anxiety has led to complex trauma in adulthood – which must be recognized and understood in order for you to survive as emotionally safely as possible. One of the absolute keys to emotional wellbeing, in my view, is knowledge. The following are the areas of knowledge that could be vital in combatting existing anxiety, especially if that anxiety comes from long-term exposure to autism-unfriendly living:

1 Knowledge of autism
2 Knowledge of the application of that knowledge
3 Knowledge of what can and can't be done about that new-found knowledge

Knowledge of autism

This might sound a bit like a no-brainer, but it so rarely gets discussed – it amazes me that it doesn't get the attention it deserves. For you as an autistic adult, my assertion is that you will not have a good understanding of your own self without an understanding of autism. Now, this is highly problematic, as much of what you read or listen to or watch about autism as a subject is likely to either be flawed, completely wrong, or inapplicable. Autism theorists abound – there are any number of autism-related journals and books, for example – but the fact that we keep writing them is an indication, by default, that we are yet to come up with any decent answers that apply across the board. I will be critiquing autism criteria later, but for now, even with a focus on autism theory, I can comfortably state that there is no autism theory that explains autism for all autistic individuals. At best, I would suggest that *some* autism theory explains *some* of the lived autistic experiences *some* of the time for *some* autistic people. This is my third suggestion for the Act:

> *A reasonable adjustment is that everyone involved in the support of an autistic person is fully aware that, at best, only* some *autism theory explains* some *of the lived autistic experiences* some *of the time for* some *autistic people.*

This puts you in a very tricky position; after all, if my assertion is valid, how are you supposed to learn anything useful about autism? My view is that an in-depth exploration of autism theory along with a critique as to which aspects of it are relevant to you as a human might be a good starting point. The problem then turns into what should you believe in the first instance? I feel that you may well be the perfect person to identify what you believe when it comes to learning about autism – but it might also be useful to engage with others whom you trust to enable you to glean an appropriate understanding – which leads me to the next stage.

Knowledge of the application of that knowledge

This ties in with the previous section; when learning about autism it might be extremely useful to identify which aspects of knowledge actually apply to you – and when. This latter aspect is vital. Nothing within autism theory is set in stone – it is highly likely that you will change over time and that what might have been applicable in terms of autism theory in the past no longer applies – and vice versa. In a similar vein, what might apply in one context may not apply in another. Anxiety will play a huge part in this – the more anxious you are, the more likely it is that certain aspects of autism theory that apply to you will become significantly problematic. So, for example, monotropism is a theory with growing popularity among the autistic population – not least as it was developed by autistic academics. Monotropism is essentially a theory that suggests that those who are monotropic will process information in single channels – so-called 'attention tunnels'. It is difficult to switch between tunnels which might explain much about the lived autistic experience which, after all, is what a good theory should be able to do.

You will be able to read all about autism theory elsewhere, but my point here is that the more anxious you are, the more you might align to being monotropic; whereas in a state of calm it might be that the impact of being monotropic lessens. It is clear to me that anxiety states are directly correlated to cognitive processing – in other words, the more anxious you are the lower your capacity to function at a high cognitive level – just one of the many reasons why it is so important to reduce anxiety, and why it is so important for anxiety states to be recognized by others as something that needs addressing to ensure that you are not disadvantaged. So – my fourth suggestion for a reasonable adjustment is as follows:

> It is recognized that the more anxious a person is, the more disadvantaged they are and the more likely it is that a reasonable adjustment is required.

Knowledge of how autism theory, or others' experiences, as documented on blogs, vlogs, Twitter etc., impact on you might go a long way towards you having an understanding of who you are as an autistic person. Key points to remember are that there are no hard and fast rules about what autism is – but there are plenty of aspects that can be challenged in terms of what autism is not. I have already outlined my stance on 'autism as a disorder' and I will come back to this later; there are other aspects that have been mooted over the years that can be challenged. My view is that if we all had a better perspective on autism, and agreed more accurately and consistently about certain aspects of autism, the more effective we would be at meeting needs. These are just my opinions with some level of justification – others are bound to disagree! This list, in no particular order, presents aspects of autism that have been discussed in autism literature and autism-related narratives over the years – and some of these are still current debates.

- Autism is not caused by bad parenting.
- Autism cannot be cured.
- Autism is not behavioural.
- Functioning labels are unhelpful, as are notions of severity.
- Being autistic has little to do with sociability.
- Being autistic doesn't mean you are no longer allowed a personality.

Autism is not caused by bad parenting

This is such an obvious one that it really shouldn't require a mention, but the prevalence of parents for whom information asserts that they are somehow to blame is still high enough to warrant its inclusion. Many parents (and you may well be among this number – after all, as an autistic adult you may well have autistic children) after their child has been identified will be encouraged to go onto a family or parenting course. This is somewhat astonishing to me – while it is not the same as the decades-old, completely disproved theory that autism was caused by so-called 'refrigerator mothers' it still smacks of parent blame to me.

Autism cannot be cured

And why should it be? I know that there are many people within society who insist that autism is a bad thing and that it causes nothing but distress to them or their child, but I remain convinced that it is not autism on its own that causes such distress. The equation I set out in Chapter 1 must also be taken into account, as must additional issues that are not part of being autistic. If, for example, a child has additional developmental and or cognitive difficulties, whatever they are, they will be a contributing factor to their wellbeing; co-occurring mental health problems, a learning disability, or any number of other difficulties may also be a part of an individual's profile – in which case it would be difficult to accept that all issues faced by the individual are down to being autistic. At the very least, it is crystal clear that there are many perfectly content autistic people out there – in which case, by definition, autism cannot always be a negative thing.

Autism is not behavioural

This one is perplexing and yet so simple. If we can acknowledge that there is no behaviour (or set of behaviours) that can be attributed to all autistic people and not to any other population, then it stands to reason that the actual notion of 'autistic behaviour' is nonsensical. And yet the narrative is commonly full of exactly that phrase – 'autistic behaviour'. Of course there are all sorts of behaviours that might be commonly found within the autistic population – but it remains that none of these are shared by all autistic people, and none of them are exclusive to the autistic population either! Autism is not a set of behaviours, and therefore there are real dangers in understanding it in that context. Just as a quick but important aside – there are always reasons behind behaviour; just because we might not understand the behaviour does not mean that there is no underlying reason for it. Understanding behaviour as communication is of paramount importance, rather than judging that behaviour through a PNT lens. Additionally, the same behaviour might be displayed either by two individuals, or even the same individual but at different times – and the reason behind it might be different for each person or circumstance.

Functioning labels are unhelpful, as are notions of severity

The notion of a spectrum which can somehow be graded from severe to mild and back again is hugely problematic. Without wishing to labour the point, once again much will depend on the environment. Current systems suggest that we should identify support levels for those identified as autistic – and yet surely those support needs will differ completely, entirely depending on circumstances. What might require high levels of support for one individual in certain circumstances may require no support whatsoever in different circumstances. Alternatively, a person may need lots of support in certain areas of life yet be an expert at providing others with support in other areas. It is very common for you to have what is referred to as a spiky profile – in other words you may be tons better at some things compared to the PNT and less able in others – while the PNT tend to be somewhat less extreme. But this should not mean that we subsequently label you in a rather binary manner when the reality is far more complicated than that. Far more beneficial is to understand yourself within any particular context at any one time.

Being autistic has little to do with sociability

I can practically hear the screams of defiance over this one – but rather than throw the book away in despair let me explain. I will cover social anxiety shortly – but sociability is something else; the need for, or desire for, social interaction (in whatever guise) relates to levels of sociability – and my view is that the spectrum of sociability, from wanting to be a loner to wanting to be a party animal, is as broad within the autistic population as within the PNT. I fully accept that more of you are likely to be less of a sociable being than wanting 24-hour social contact – but that doesn't preclude it as a possibility.

Being autistic doesn't mean you are no longer allowed a personality

It sometimes seems to me that as soon as autism is mentioned one is no longer allowed a personality. I wrote a blog entry on this (see the Further reading page), based on a parent who told me about how fed up she was when people seemed shocked that her children were autistic because 'they are so lovely' – as if having a lovely personality meant that one could not be autistic.

So – getting back to how you might better understand your own anxiety states. I have covered the triangle of facets that you may take into account, but there are other means that might be useful to consider as well – an additional three, which are:

- Symptoms
- Comparative emotional states
- Levels of exhaustion.

Symptoms

Anxiety might not obviously manifest itself in behaviour – masking is highly prevalent in autism and I will cover it later. However, anxiety, while hidden to the outside world, may be indicated at a physical level that you can identify. The obvious indication of anxiety is an increased heart rate. You may be someone who is acutely aware of your heart rate in which case it is well worth monitoring, to ascertain whether changes in it can help identify levels of anxiety. However, some of you may have sensory hyposensitivity specific to interoception (which relates to processing and understanding sensations from within your body, such as feeling hungry) in which case you may not be as aware of your own heart rate as others. Technology can be really useful here – heart rate monitors are not particularly expensive, and many smart watches these days come with the technology that can identify and track things like your pulse. Having a 24-hour tracking device to ascertain heart rate could be useful – not least to identify whether your anxiety levels could be identified using such a system, but also to work out whether on average you tend to be more anxious than the general population. Of course there does need to be a word of caution here – it would be mindful to involve a health professional in terms of understanding what the data actually means.

You might find that it is possible to identify other symptoms of anxiety other than your heart rate. Anxiety is so individual there is no 'one size fits all', so being conscious of other physical aspects that might indicate anxiety, such as sweating, shaking, or increased sensory sensitivities, is well worth thinking about.

Comparative emotional states

While it is not always easy to answer the question 'How do you feel?', it is much easier to work out how you feel in comparison to how you felt an hour ago, or yesterday, or last week. Sometimes it is beneficial simply to work out what trajectory you are on – are you feeling better on the whole than before (in which case something is going right), or are things getting worse? When you are anxious it can feel as though nothing will change, and you will never feel anxiety-free again – and yet gradually, over a period of time, if the environment changes to better suit your needs, it could be that you think back and realize that a week has passed and there is a difference in how you feel.

Levels of exhaustion

Being anxious takes its toll. The more anxious you are, the more energy you are likely to be using up – so sometimes keeping track of how exhausted you are on a day-to-day basis might help indicate levels of anxiety. Sleep patterns are also very likely to be affected – so a sleep and exhaustion diary may be beneficial if you wanted to work out if there are patterns to anxiety.

Of course you may well be hyper-aware of your own anxiety, in which case none of this will be necessary! Many of you will be only too well aware of how anxious you feel and simply (ha – as if it were simple!) want to do something about it.

Social anxiety

While you may feel anxious in any number of situations, one of the main ones that is so common among autistic adults is the oft-dreaded social scene. Simply being with people – and by 'people' I am referring to those outside of the usually small numbers of folk you feel absolutely safe with – can increase anxiety. A note to those reading this who do not usually suffer from social anxiety – by social anxiety I am referring to conscious levels of anxiety, often accompanied by physical symptoms (that you might not even notice yourself) to the point of it detracting from the ability to function. It is categorically not the mild anxiety that is sometimes felt by the PNT on infrequent occasions. It is so frustrating when you disclose that you are socially anxious and the response – well-meaning though it may be – is something along the lines of, 'Yes, I get a bit anxious too', when the reality is very different indeed. Being anxious to the point of actual debilitation is not the same as feeling slightly socially awkward or uncomfortable.

> Imagine one of the most stressful situations that you have been in. Maybe speaking at a public event, maybe a major exam, maybe a job interview, maybe a presentation to work colleagues, maybe that time you got lost as a child and couldn't find your parents in the supermarket. Think about how that made you feel – quite possibly you felt sick, your ability to think went out of the proverbial window, you might even have been close to panic. You would quite likely have very happily swopped that experience for something – anything – less anxiety-inducing at that point in time. Ok – so you recall those feelings?

Now imagine that you experience a version of this every single time you enter a room that has other people in it. Imagine if this is how you feel when you have to go to the work social do. Imagine this is how you feel when you have to visit the in-laws.

If you don't experience that level of anxiety in what most people would regard as every day, usual occurrences that are not particularly prominent in any way, then it is likely that you will be unable to empathize with someone who is socially anxious.

It is hard writing this – it sounds as though I might be having a bit of a go at people who are trying their best to be kind; however, if you do not share those feelings of anxiety within social situations, pretending that you do or inferring that your experiences are somehow comparable can come across as patronizing – even offensive.

Social anxiety, then, is related to social occasions – in other words any occasion that involves another person or other people. What many folk don't realize is that social anxiety is not exclusively aligned with physically being present in a social event. Included within social anxiety are:

• Social communication outside of face-to-face
• Ruminating on past social events
• Thinking about social situations that are yet to occur.

Social communication outside of face-to-face

This refers to aspects of life such as phone calls, texts, online activity, thank you cards after Christmas – and everything in between. The point is that just because an activity does not involve direct physical contact, it doesn't mean that it can't induce social anxiety. In fact, sometimes the anxiety is even worse, especially if there are time delays involved (see Chapter 4).

Ruminating on past social events

It is so, so common for you to ruminate on past social events, sometimes years later. This seems to involve trying to work out what could have gone better, why things have gone the way that they did, and what could have been changed to make the situation less problematic. This kind of rumination, which may impact massively on ongoing anxiety, is such a common theme. Some of you may even relive aspects of anxiety that you felt in the past when thinking about those events, as if you were actually still there.

Thinking about social situations that are yet to occur

Again, this may well be a common theme for you. Knowing that an event is going to happen, and that you are inevitably going to be a part of it, may cause ongoing thoughts about it that increase anxiety levels. Wondering just how it will play out, what impact it will have on you, what impact you might have on others – these are all aspects that take up precious emotional energy that many people will never understand.

Meltdowns/shutdowns

Many of you will be all too familiar with one or both of these. Anxiety will frequently reach a point whereby there is a physical reaction that cannot be controlled by you. Some of you may only ever have meltdowns, others may only have shutdowns, some of you may experience both. For those readers who do not experience either, please understand that they can both be as draining and stressful as each other – one is not 'better' or 'worse' an experience, though the outcome of individual situations can often be more impactful than others; usually (but not always) meltdowns bring a higher risk of negative repercussions compared to shutdowns, but this is not inevitably the case.

The next section is for readers who do not experience the results of ongoing, intense anxiety.

Inevitability. That is the word I request that you keep at the forefront of your minds whenever you think about a meltdown/shutdown. Actually, there are three words I would request that you are consciously aware of:

- Inevitability
- Control
- Blame.

Inevitability

Imagine something that might be slow moving, or that takes time to develop. Think of a huge pan full to the brim of water that is set over a fire to boil, or a glacier sliding down a mountain, or a volcano that might takes years to erupt. The path for each of these three scenarios is set – and by set, I mean that the outcome is inevitable: the kettle will eventually boil; the glacier will eventually destroy the village in its path; the volcano will eventually erupt.

These are just three examples – feel free to make up your own! If we understand that we can't stop the water over the fire heating to boiling point, that we cannot change the fact that the glacier will continue moving, that the volcano will erupt as a natural part of its cycle – then we can come a bit closer to understanding that if an autistic adult is on a similar pathway as a result of ongoing anxiety, then the outcome is going to be inevitable. There may be slight things that the person can do to stave off the end result, there may be things that others can do to stave off the end result – but until the very nature of the life scenario changes, the result will remain inevitable.

This latter point is one that must be taken into consideration – because it is where the examples provided as analogies no longer apply. It would be pessimistic indeed to make the assumption that meltdowns/shutdowns have to be an inevitable part of autistic life. However, my point is that if you have suffered from a meltdown/shutdown – then at that point in time it would have been inevitable. You might have delayed it in some ways, but the result was on the cards. Until we change the environment around what is causing those situations, there will be an ongoing inevitability – which is why it is so crucially important to take those environmental aspects into account.

Control

As described in the inevitability section above, you might have some limited control over the situation – the point being that your control is limited. By definition, you do not have full control in relation to meltdown/shutdown, otherwise they could be avoided.

What is incredibly frustrating is that just because there might be some small measure of control that might delay a situation, some people assume that this is the equivalent to being able to control your own emotional state in its fullest sense. This is simply not a valid argument. You may feel so anxious at work that you have to have daily meltdowns, but you are able to keep this from happening until you get to the safety of you own home, for example. You have limited control – but the meltdown is still inevitable. Of course, what often happens in this situation is that others simply either don't believe that there is an issue at work, or make the erroneous assumption that you are 'managing' your anxiety to an acceptable degree.

Anyone who has experienced states of meltdown/shutdown will know that they can be acutely stressful whatever the circumstances – but can be exacerbated if experienced within a public arena – hence why you might do everything in your power to keep it from occurring until you are away from the public eye. This is categorically not the same as having total control.

Blame

As a direct result of the combination of inevitability and control, we simply have to accept that you are not to be in any way blamed for the emotional crash that is a meltdown/shutdown. In fact, a crash is as good a way as any to use as an analogy. If you crash your car because there had been an oil spill, and the oil spill was not highlighted by any warning signs, should you be blamed for it in any way? Is driving a car in and of itself the reason for the crash – or is it the combination of the driving and the oil spill – in other words, the environment played its part in the crash, which could not be avoided. Take the oil spill out of the equation – not a problem!

Repercussions of meltdown/shutdown

Meltdowns and shutdowns should not be avoided. Wait – read on! What *should* be avoided at all costs are the causes for them occurring in the first place. If, however, anxiety *is* being experienced that leads inevitably to an emotional crash, then what needs to be done is managing that crash to the best of our ability. Trust me – I would prefer it if you didn't crash at all, but if it is not yet possible to manage the environment to deter anxiety just yet, we need to understand what these emotional crashes are, and how to work with them.

In a sense I would prefer not to distinguish between meltdowns and shutdowns, as both can be equally as traumatic – but just to be clear for everyone, both will occur when anxiety becomes overwhelming – either as a result of a specific trigger or a combination of events. When you reach the point of no return you will enter what all will be aware of as a 'fight or flight' response. I suggest that it may not be particularly useful to assume that fight equates to a meltdown and flight equates to a shutdown – again, this indicates some level of choice or control – but some people find it useful to think about meltdowns and shutdowns in those terms. I find it easier simply to distinguish between the two in relation to direction – which is either outward (meltdown) or inward (shutdown). Most meltdowns are outward manifesting – in other words those present will be able to clearly see a person in distress. Most shutdowns are inward manifesting – this can still be observed, but is usually far less obvious.

Just a quick but eminently important point regarding terms here. In fact I think it should be the fifth reasonable adjustment, stating:

If an autistic person is suffering from an emotional crash (often referred to as a meltdown) always consider using the term 'distressed' behaviour rather than the more common terms such as 'challenging' or even 'aggressive' or 'violent'.

The impact on changing terminology could be significant. I am not suggesting for one moment that an autistic adult is excluded from behaving in a way that could be referred to as, for example, aggressive. However, behaviour as a result of a meltdown should never be regarded as anything other than distressed behaviour, irrespective of how it might be exhibited. I would suggest that changing the terms would mean there is reduced risk of supporting the individual in the wrong way; changing the term to make it clear that the behaviour is as a direct result of distress could change the perspective of those around him/her as to how the individual could best be supported. So, to reiterate, irrespective of what the actual behaviour is – if it is as direct result of a meltdown, it should never be regarded as 'challenging', and always within the context of 'distress'.

So, a meltdown might result in certain behaviours being exhibited; a shutdown tends to be more along the lines of uncontrollable withdrawal – in whatever form that might take. It may mean that you are no longer able to process information, speak, engage with the outside world; it could take the form of extreme exhaustion, loss of energy, and/or loss of function.

These emotional crashes do serve a purpose – rather like a valve letting off steam, they counterbalance the intense anxiety that has been experienced, and – in some cases but not always – almost recalibrate you. This is not to suggest for one moment that we should be accepting or encouraging emotional crashes – but we should recognize that a constant search to avoid the inevitable is not the way forward; the only way forward that holds any appeal to me is to identify the causes of anxiety on an individual basis, and subsequently eliminate them.

In terms of the repercussions for you, while there might be some level of recalibration, it is far more likely that the impact in the main will be negative. So many of you will have had some level of blame – even punishment – for having an emotional crash. The sooner we realize that your emotional crashes are not in your control and subsequently eliminate all blame, the better for your mental wellbeing.

Tips for those who care about you and/or who are part of your support

1. Firstly, as noted, do everything in your power to reduce the need for an emotional crash in the first instance – in other words, eliminate anxiety wherever and whenever possible.

2. Make sure that the person and anyone else present is safe, but never assume that physical control over the person (i.e. restraint) should ever be a preferred option unless there is literally no other way to keep safe. Restraint should not only be a last resort, it should be rare in the extreme – and even then, we should be working out a way for it never to happen again. If restraint is being used with any frequency at all during emotional crashes then we have absolutely got the environment wrong and it needs urgent attention.

3. Do as much homework as possible prior to the crash – when in the throes of an emotional crash one of the last things to expect is some kind of detailed discussion as to what a person's preferences might be – getting this information during a time of calm is infinitely a better option.

4. If a person is experiencing an emotional crash, do as much as possible to take any pressure off that person, whatever that might be. For some this could be not expecting them to engage, for others it might be that being on their own in a safe place is the best option.

5. Take as much attention off the person as possible – having a focus on you while you're at your most vulnerable can be agonizing.

6. While taking note of point four, bear in mind that some people will be greatly reassured by the presence of a trusted 'safe' person.

7. Take as much control over the situation as the person requires – it will be easier for a person to get through an emotional crash without having to make ongoing decisions themselves so long as someone else can make the right decisions on their behalf.

8. Remember that sensory experiences might well be heightened during an emotional crash – so make sure that you have an understanding of sensory needs at these times.

9. Never appoint blame or indicate that the emotional crash is anything other than an inevitable culmination of anxiety caused by the environment.

10. Recognize the amount of time that a person needs to recover, and provide the time and space to do so.
11. Never put pressure on a person to come out of an emotional crash until they are ready to do so – remember, the individual is not in control and being encouraged to 'snap out of it' is likely to cause more damage than is already being done.
12. Recognize that the person is likely to feel extremely vulnerable during and after an emotional crash – reassurance and reiteration of a no blame culture could be significantly important here.

These are guidelines rather than hard-and-fast rules – though some individual points could be applied across the board. Emotional crashes are individual experiences, and should be understood from an individual perspective.

When might you crash?

Some people experience frequent emotional crashes of differing degrees, but what is not necessarily acknowledged within the common narrative relating to autism and age, is that there are certainly some individuals for whom years of living with anxiety without any meltdown/shutdown eventually leads to a massive episode that might even be misunderstood within the context of psychiatric illness. I remain convinced that we are a long way off from understanding this, but I am very well aware of some individuals who have shared with me that what had originally been diagnosed as a psychiatric 'breakdown' (and terms will differ) in hindsight it had become clear that they had suffered a massive meltdown or shutdown after decades of anxiety. Sometimes these episodes have a discernible trigger – a major lifestyle change (retirement, bereavement, or moving home are all real-life examples that I have been made aware of) but not always. As noted, we are a long way off really understanding anxiety in older adults, but this kind of emotional crash certainly needs to be recognized to reduce the chances of a harmful misunderstanding as to what is happening.

Long-term impact of anxiety

As noted right at the start of the book, long-term anxiety has very real, very significant, and often life-altering consequences. It cannot be reiterated enough (ok, maybe I labour the point – but that's how important it is) – that we *must* do everything we can to avoid anxiety in general, but long-term ongoing anxiety has to become a thing of the past as a priority. It is pretty obvious what the long-term implications might be for you – the impact on wellbeing and levels of being content can be insufferable. However, there are also the health implications to take into account.

I am not a medic – I am not clinically trained in any area, in fact. However, I am not in the least bit surprised at the numbers of you who report health issues such as chronic fatigue or fibromyalgia. The impact that being in an ongoing state of fight or flight, without actually being able to do either most of the time, must surely increase the chances of there being a physiological outcome.

Don't cope with anxiety

One of the most frustrating concepts in my view is that teaching you to cope with anxiety is somehow a positive thing. Surely the aim should be taking anxiety out of the equation rather than putting the responsibility on you simply to cope with it? I absolutely understand that coping mechanisms can be a very positive thing in certain circumstances – but they should never be used when an elimination of the anxiety-inducing environment is an option instead. In fact, there is still a feeling within society it seems to me that being anxious is and should somehow be your emotional state to own and, therefore, do something about. This is not far off understanding anxiety from a medical model perspective, as opposed to understanding that we all have a part to play in the reduction of anxiety for humankind, and we should take ownership collectively to do so.

3
Sensory issues

I have written elsewhere about sensory issues (see the Further reading page), so I am mindful that I don't simply want to re-write what you could access elsewhere (including a free blog on sensory issues, so don't feel that you have to buy another book of mine!). Suffice to say, though, we need to have an understanding that sensory experiences are pervasive and impactful, and there can certainly be a link between sensory experiences and anxiety. In many cases the environment equation (see Chapter 1) can be taken quite literally – the physical environment can have a very real impact on anxiety that needs to be recognized and understood on an individual basis.

Essentially, you are very likely to experience hyper sensory and/or hyposensory (i.e. over or under sensitive in comparison to others) sensitivities in any or all of your eight senses. Simply, you will have a sensory profile that is often quite different compared to most of the PNT. Knowing what that is – both you and others who are involved with you – and subsequent changes in the environment can go a long way to a more stable sensory environment that, in turn, can go a long way towards a reduction of ongoing anxiety.

Even though you may be able to develop a sensory profile, never forget that it is not set in stone! There are all sorts of influencing factors involved in your sensory experience, not least your current emotional state. So what this means is that even when you have worked out, in a general sense, what your sensory profile might look like, you will need to acknowledge that it might differ over time, or within different environments – or, even, with different people. Knowledge is power – and having an acute understanding of self when it comes to sensory experiences can be seriously advantageous. One of the things that I am frequently reminded of is just how many of you may not know that your sensory experiences differ in any way compared either to other autistic adults or the PNT – I mean, why would you know? Unless you proactively seek out where your sensory life is on a day-to-day basis, you may not be cognizant that it differs widely to most other people. Until you have a grasp of how the sensory world is treating you, you may not be in a position to do anything about it.

The fact is that much of the physical environment will be set up to suit the majority of those accessing it – with some exceptions, of course. Those exceptions, in the main, will not be suited to you though! Autism hour in supermarkets aside, how much of society's environments take your sensory needs into account? I suspect that because of the range of autistic sensory experiences that exist, it might be impossible to expect society to adapt to such a degree that all environments suit all autistic people – in which case your individual circumstances and changing what is necessary for you to be anxiety free becomes the goal. So not all employers need to get rid of open-plan offices, but yours might need to consider how to partition your area off, or provide you with an alternative safe space. Not all of the carriages on trains need to be quiet zones – but there should be access to a carriage that is not a quiet zone, but a silent zone – and this is consistently monitored to ensure that the rule is enforced. Not all supermarkets need to have a one-way system so that those of you who are tactile sensitive to others need not fear having a stranger brush past you – but during autism hour there is a system in place to ensure that you feel safe.

The point is that, while the task of making the world a sensory suitable place for you might seem so onerous as to be impossible, the reality is that we can go an awful long way to ensuring that at least most of your needs are met, at least to some degree. Of the three examples above, I don't think any of them are too much to ask – I would go as far as to suggest that each of them could be seen as reasonable adjustments in many cases – so while we won't be able to adjust every environment to meet every need, we can make huge strides towards providing safe sensory environments at least some of the time for many or even most of you.

As already noted, your emotional state will impact on your sensory experiences – and vice versa. Ongoing exposure to the wrong sensory environment can (and likely will) trigger anxiety that will have a longer-term detrimental impact. That is one of the fundamental reasons why sensory needs must be taken seriously into consideration.

Imagine for a moment that you live in terror of someone unexpectedly knocking on your door – which is the reality for some people I know. Society refuses to do anything about this, and you are left in a constant state of anxiety arousal, because most of society cannot comprehend just how terrifying it is. Compare this with a system whereby it becomes commonplace to have an indication on your doorway that unless it is absolutely necessary for there to be a knock at the door, alternative arrangements must be made. It's interesting to note that as I am writing this, what used to be common practice (signing for a parcel, which used to be mandatory) has now almost completely disappeared and a new system has taken its place. It occurs to me that very often these step changes in living are seen as insurmountable until such a time when the PNT require the changes – at which point they occur more or less seamlessly.

This isn't to apportion blame – but if we as a society understood just how negatively impactful living in fear of a knock at the door might be for someone, maybe we would be more inclined simply to make those appropriate changes. I am not suggesting that the knock on the door is the most terrible sensory experience for most of you – but it is an example of how society can impact on you – negatively or, with change, positively.

Change in sensory environments, then, is essential if we are going to proactively reduce anxiety. But it is important to note that sensory profiles are not preferences – they are actual needs. It's not that you are being fussy wanting your own space at work; it is because you can only operate at 50 per cent efficiency while being in a constant state of stress in the exposure of an open plan office. It's not just that it might be more pleasant to sit on a train where noise has been banned, and the rule is enforced; it's a case of not being able to use the train at all. It's not that you simply prefer to have a one-way system when out shopping – it's because having a stranger brush past you is intensely painful. Ignoring the need for sensory change, in some (possibly many, or even the majority of) cases, may well be unlawful. If a sensory experience puts you at a substantial disadvantage, and it would be reasonable to make an adjustment to suit your needs – then surely it could be considered unlawful not to do so? This is problematic when applied across the whole of society, but on an individual basis it is well worth considering. I believe, in fact, that we should also be considering reasonable adjustments on a global scale within society at the same time, to at least reduce the risk of discrimination. The example of train carriages might be one to consider as a genuine reasonable adjustment. And for those of you reading this who feel that the 'quiet carriage' is sufficient, please reconsider. If anything, the fact that they are labelled as 'quiet' and almost always are anything but, makes for an experience that could be even worse than going to the carriage that is *not* exempt from noise – while that might be sensory hell for you, at least you don't have to put up with people breaking the rules.

Before going on to identifying some of the potential sensory triggers for anxiety, I will take the opportunity to provide a brief example as to how society seems to 'brand' you as in some way inferior – and in this example clearly gets it wrong. My rationale for including this is just to provide yet another example of how, if we educated ourselves better, we could dramatically improve the lives of autistic adults, simply by not 'getting it wrong' – which, on a personal note, is frustrating at best, and downright anxiety-inducing at other times. Much of the autism narrative refers to delayed processing – the argument being that you take longer to process the same information as the PNT. While this might be the case for some, it absolutely is not the case for many. It may well *appear* that you are taking longer to process information, but the reality is that you are consciously processing way more than the PNT – so the overall impression is that of a delay. In fact, you might be processing information at a *faster* rate than the PNT – but because you have so much to process due to your exceptional sensory skills, it has the effect of delaying the overall experience. Consider the following:

> Ethan is not chosen to go forward to the next stage of the interview process. The panel has convened and all are agreed that while his

responses were absolutely apt, the delay he took in responding to the questions meant that he was considered unsuitable for the job, even though the job itself does not involve verbal communication. The actual job is advertised as working from home, in isolation. Ethan's reality is that he has an acute sensory sensitivity to both visual and auditory information. He has declared this on his application form, and as a result the employer decided that to try and make life fair they would dim the lights and turn the air conditioning unit off. Ethan has to sit in a room that from his perspective is sensorily overwhelming – from the colour of the carpet and the pictures on the wall to the cacophony of noises coming from the rest of the building and the ambulance siren going off a mile away – and everything, pretty much, in between. He has to process dozens of sensory stimuli at any given time, while still making the extraordinary effort to listen to the questions being put to him, digest them, and provide an answer. He is processing at a far greater speed than the average person is ever able to achieve, and yet comes across as having difficulty in responding to questions. He rather wishes that the panel had simply done as he had asked in the first place, which was to allow him to be interviewed from home via video link – after all, that would have been his working environment if he had been successful in the interview process. As usual, Ethan feels rather frustrated with life, and wonders what his prospects will ever be.

This is an example in which processing speeds might appear to be one thing, but in reality are very different – and yet the lasting impression of the autistic adult is that they are too slow. These examples of lack of understanding and, therefore, a cause for anxiety – are, I believe, an every day occurrence for many of you. Let's go for suggested reasonable adjustment six:

> When an autistic person tells you how they experience a sensory environment, make every attempt to believe them and take it seriously, irrespective as to whether you share that experience or not.

Essentially what I am suggesting here – and, let's face it, it's not rocket science, though you may be mistaken for thinking it is seeing how often it's ignored – is that it would be a very good idea for society to actually listen to you and what you believe your sensory needs are. Many of you will be well aware as to what causes you distress within the sensory world and are perfectly willing and able to share those thoughts; and yet, on many occasions, society seems to prefer to ignore you.

. I have written about sensory experiences in other narratives – here I will just give some examples related to some of the issues that might be worth considering as a starting point. The following is not an exhaustive list of all of the components of sensory issues that are required for consideration – they are just some examples of what could make a difference to some of you. A note to the PNT here – many of the PNT will not share the sensory profiles of the autistic adult; but just because there is not a shared experience does not detract from the very real experiences of the autistic adult. Simply, if an autistic person shares a sensory experience with you, assume that it is absolutely real – however far-fetched that seems at the time. I remember very clearly the first time I came across sensory sensitivity in the autism world, when someone I was working with told me just how painful each individual drop of water was when having a shower – describing each droplet as being akin to a pinprick, and the torrent of water as a waterfall of pins. I was absolutely astounded – and shocked, as I had never heard of such a thing before. Since then I have learned that most of you will have sensory stories to tell, and that they need to be taken seriously, however little others might be able to empathize with them. The problem is that some people appear to have problems with some of the more extreme sensory sensitivities that you may experience – they simply cannot accept that they are just as valid a sensory experience as anyone else's, autistic or not. So, I have included some real-life sensory experiences to try and persuade the PNT that from a sensory perspective, many of you will differ quite considerably to the majority of the PNT.

Auditory

Extreme hypersensitivity

Some of you will have hearing abilities that can seem super-human to many of the PNT. This is problematic in many ways, not least the fact that others may struggle to identify what you can hear when they can't themselves. I have known you to hear noises such as helicopters several miles away, or sirens that are way beyond the usual range of auditory ability.

> Felicity is able to identify the noise of an airplane from several miles away. Not only can she hear the noise of the plane as it is taking off, she can identify the make and model of the plane by the sound of its engine. Remarkably, no one else in her house can hear any noise at all – and yet when Felicity tells them the make and model of the plane, and they follow her outside, when they eventually see the plane she is always proven right.

There so many other examples, some of them just as extraordinary – which many of you will live with on a day-to-day basis.

Hyperacusis

This is the term used to describe hypersensitivity to specific noises that may often be painful to you, whereas many others will either not notice them or not find them unpleasant in any way. These can be split into specific areas that are all worth considering (the list is not exclusive nor exhaustive):

- Sudden noises
- Specific noises
- Humming-type noise
- Background noise
- Noise in general.

Sudden noises

These could also be described as unexpected noise, or noise that it is not possible to ascertain exactly when it might happen. Fireworks are a superb example of this – some of you will find the noise of fireworks difficult to process, even painful. A firework that goes off when totally unexpected might cause more difficulty than a firework going off during a celebration or festival in which fireworks are commonplace – however, as it is still unpredictable, it can still cause a problem. Other examples might include a dog barking, or a baby crying.

Specific noises

This takes individuality into account, and relates to very specific noises that you might find problematic. Also known as misophonia, some of you might find a certain noise troublesome in a range of severity – from annoying all the way through to terrifying. This might change over time, or from one context to the next. As with many sensory profiles it may well also change depending on your emotional state.

Humming-type noise

I think that this is worth a category in its own right – the sort of noise that an air-conditioning unit makes, or a vacuum cleaner, or a wind turbine – these are all examples of humming-type noise that some of you will find distracting to the point of not being able to function within their vicinity.

Background noise

Some of you will pick up on noise within your setting irrespective of its volume. In that sense, what others might regard as background noise could simply all come under the umbrella of 'noise'. It's poignant to note that many of the PNT will be able to empathize with this when it's pointed out that, when they feel stressed in the car (e.g. they are lost), many people will turn the volume down on the radio to avoid the distraction. However, some of you will experience these distractions in all settings. The ticking of the clock could be just as noticeable to you as the person who is speaking to you. Or, the person chatting at the far end of the room is just as audible as the person speaking with you who is sat next to you. It doesn't take much to realize just how problematic these experiences will be, in so many settings. Some of you will find that noise cancelling headphones are suitable to allow you to exist in an environment where there is a lot of distracting background noise; however, these will not be effective for everyone, so while they might be a useful consideration, they should not be an automatic 'go-to' solution for all of you who might have auditory sensitivities.

Noise in general

Perhaps less common than was previously thought, though equally as important as any other auditory sensitivity, some of you will simply find noise – whatever the source – problematic. This is more related to volume – but please be aware that any of you might have issues around anything included in the list.

Olfactory

Your sense of smell is one of those areas that often seems to get missed, and yet it can be just as impactful as any of the other senses. As within the auditory domain, some of you will have a sense of smell that is extraordinarily heightened – I know people who can tell a person's identity by their individual smell, those who can smell 'essence' of a person on a chair several hours after it has been vacated, the ability to pick up on subtle smells that others can never consciously process. Some issues to consider include:

- The smell of animals
- Smells that offend
- Overwhelming smells.

The smell of animals

Never underestimate the gloriousness that some of you will find in the smell of certain animals – sometimes a specific pet, sometimes a species in general. Dogs and horses can smell so utterly delightful that a single sniff can balance out a day that has been hard. Dogs and horses are just a couple of examples – a freshly windswept cat can be of equal value, for example. Sometimes it might be a specific area of the animal – dog's paws and muzzles spring immediately to mind, or it might be that the dog needs to have existed in a particular environment to perfect their olfactory delight – imagine the utter joy of sniffing a dog's paws after it has had a paddle in a clean running river, and then gently dried them in the summer sun – ok, this is rather specific, but you get my point!

Smells that offend

Some smells, in a similar way to the examples of noise given previously, can be offensive – or even painful – on an individual basis. Hyperosmia – the general term for a heightened sense of smell – identifies that there might be specific smells that can impact extremely negatively on you. Examples might include perfume, cleaning products, candles, essential oils – frustratingly for many of you, the smells that might cause a problem might be the exact same smell that others find pleasant. What is absolutely clear is that your sense of smell might be so acute that individual offensive smells can literally be the difference between whether or not you can access a certain space.

Overwhelming smells

Some smells – and this will be linked to hyperosmia – will be so intense or 'blanket' that they can be overwhelming. In such cases it may be that there is a direct impact on your levels of anxiety; it is incredibly important that you are able to identify and remove such situations from your life as much as is humanly possible. The sense of smell is one that so many take for granted as something that rarely causes a problem, but for you it might be a daily source of discomfort. The removal of overwhelming smells and/or offensive smells *will* influence your wellbeing, so it is vital that they are recognized and dealt with if circumstances allow.

Visual

Some of the areas that are important to consider – either because there are myths associated with them, or because they can be so impactful – include:

- Eye contact
- Lighting
- Too much stimuli
- Noticing the detail
- Loving visual patterns
- Visual thinker rather than verbal.

These are not in the slightest bit exclusive – but hopefully give some 'flavour' as to what thought needs to go into understanding the visual sensory profiles that some of you may have.

Eye contact

This one is pretty easy to write about – and yet still, to this day, there is resistance within society to take the issue as seriously as it needs to be for some (many) of you. Quite simply, for many of you, eye contact will range from being uncomfortable to distracting, from distressing to painful. Many of you (possibly all) *can* give eye contact, maintain eye contact, and appear to have a similar use of eye contact to the PNT. Appearances can be deceptive though! Some of you will have worked out alternatives that give the effect of direct eye contact even though there is no eye contact at all (e.g. looking at a person's mouth, or nose). Others will have eye contact but be in a state of high distress as a result. Others will have eye contact but in doing so will not be able to focus on anything else. Others will have eye contact because they have been taught to do so even though it causes great discomfort. Others will appear to use eye contact in the same way as the PNT – with the assumption being that you will glean the same (non-verbal) information when in fact you gain nothing at all.

The reality is that if the following is applicable to you, then it might be well worth considering what the point of eye contact actually is. Are you someone who:

- finds eye contact painful?
- finds eye contact distracting?
- finds eye contact a waste of time?
- understands that eye contact should be made to make others feel comfortable, even when it makes you feel uncomfortable?
- finds eye contact overwhelming?
- feels that having to give eye contact means that all your energy is taken just by doing so?

If the answer to any of these is 'yes', then I would suggest that you seek an alternative. Some of the PNT will insist that you need to have direct eye contact in order to do all sorts of things, such as maintain attention, understand non-verbal cues, give non-verbal cues, give a good impression – these may well all be an accurate assumption when related to the PNT – but those reasons may well not apply to you, in which case alternatives are usually a far better option.

For the PNT – please don't insist on eye contact from an autistic person who finds it distressing. For some, forced eye contact detracts from the ability to process relevant information (such as your voice). For others, it is akin to abuse. There are a whole range of negative states in between – irrespective of the specific, if the downside of direct eye contact outweighs any perceived benefits (and we have to ask ourselves if the autistic person is ever the beneficiary) then surely it would be only fair to avoid it.

Lighting

Ok – so the one lots of people will be aware of is the dreaded fluorescent light strip, but make no mistake this is (by far) not the only aspect of lighting that can cause a problem. Fluorescent lighting flickers at a speed that most people cannot discern (until they are wearing out) and also makes a buzzing noise – both can be incredibly distracting if you can see and/or hear the light. Not only that, but the harsh glare of the light can also be something that your eyes may find incredibly difficult to process.

Unnatural (electric) light as a whole tends to be more problematic compared to natural light – gas lighting and candles, for example, have been reported to me by some as far better than electric light. Of electric lighting, some of the glow of energy-saving bulbs can be a huge issue, while other electric lights can be a delight. As is so often the case, your reactions and needs will differ to someone else – experimentation can be a very useful process to go through when it comes to lighting; some of you will get tension headaches with the 'wrong' lighting, while the 'right' lighting will assist in a sense of peace.

Too much stimuli

The world is a busy place, and many environments are visually stimulating. Having the ability to process huge amounts of visual data at the same time can be extraordinary, but it can also be overwhelming and overbearing. Detailed wallpaper can have the effect of stopping other senses operate, whereas plain painted walls could be far more beneficial. Busy displays can be distracting at best, while simply uncluttered environments could provide energy and useful stimulation. Of course, as usual – each to their own! But it is definitely worth considering what type of visual environment best suits you, and at what times.

Noticing the detail

Many of you will be expert at noticing the detail; many of you will also (contrary to popular belief) be very good at seeing the collection of the detail as well. Some of you will be very good at identifying detail and have to work harder at processing the gestalt. Visual processing styles can make a huge difference to what visual environment best suits you, so having a good understanding of what is best suited to you (and when) is of potential benefit.

Loving visual patterns/uniformity

Some of you will be extremely adept at identifying visual patterns, uniformity, symmetry, and so on – but this wonderful ability can also cause problems if the environment is not 'correct'. Pictures that are not hung straight, adjacent tables that are not lined up in parallel, or lines of chairs at the conference that are askew – all sorts of situations such as these can distract and irritate to the point of causing anxiety.

Visual thinker rather than verbal

It is untrue to declare all of you as visual thinkers – but there does seem to be a preference for visual thinking styles over verbal compared to the PNT. This can help in all sorts of roles, but it can also detract from processing if visual information is not readily available. It is always worth identifying what processing style suits you, and to ensure as much as possible that information is provided in a style that best suits you.

Tactile

You may be hypersensitive or hyposensitive to touch – or, far more frequently I believe, both. This can seem confusing to the

PNT who is usually one or the other, but it is common for you to have a more diverse range of tactile sensations compared to many others. This is another area that it might be difficult for those who do not share your sensations to touch to empathize with – and yet it is absolutely critical that you are understood and accommodated. I find that this is one of the areas in which you are least believed – possibly because of that lack of shared experience, or maybe because it is simply too difficult for others to genuinely empathize with what it is that you report. I don't think in this instance that empathy should be something that you seek in order to be taken seriously; if someone else is literally unable to process touch in the same way as you, it stands to reason that they will be unable to empathize. However, lacking empathy should not lead to lacking in sympathy, or the understanding that different humans experience life in different ways. I will never know the (oft-reported) pain of childbirth, but I can absolutely accept that for most women it is an extremely painful experience. Just because the PNT may never experience light touch as significantly painful, does not mean that it should be taken any less seriously. If anything, this is where your voice should be sought after as much as in any other area of life – to ascertain what levels of pain you might be in, within your tactile environment.

Proximity to others

It can be painful to be in close proximity to others – and there is a sliding scale, all the way through to mild discomfort. This is probably a combination of senses for some of you (e.g. touch and smell) but for others it might be tactile on its own.

Light touch

Light touch – simply put – can be processed as pain. Some of you will respond incredibly favourably to deep pressure, while detesting the sensation of light touch. Of course – as with all things sensory – some of you may process sensation in the reverse of this, and crave light touch. However, for those of you for whom light touch is problematic, you need to be in environments in which this is catered for, otherwise you risk being in a situation whereby you are, by default, in fight or flight mode.

> Gerraint is extremely sensitive to touch; he works in an environment in which his colleagues are very sociable, and work hard to include everyone in the same way. They are a tactile bunch and think nothing of putting a hand on a colleague's shoulder when making or point, or providing support. Gerraint sits at his desk in a state of emotional arousal that could be described as one level lower than panic, because he is aware that at any moment a co-worker might come to him from behind and rest a hand on his shoulder while speaking to him.

While this might sound like an outlandish example, it by no means is. Tactility in relation to pressure – human or otherwise – is an area that deserves the utmost attention.

Touch – light or otherwise – may also be experienced in different ways in different parts of the body. You may shudder at the mere thought of a limp handshake, and yet love the soles of your feet being brushed lightly. You may hate your upper arm being squeezed, and yet crave the deepest hug imaginable.

Deep pressure

So – in line with deep hugging – deep pressure is something that you might find incredibly soothing and relaxing. Not all of you, of course – but plenty of you will enjoy deep pressure so long as you are in control of it, at least to an extent that suits you. This may be pertinent some of the time and not others, or for some parts of the body and not others.

Clothing

Many of you will intensely dislike certain clothes – be it texture, tightness, looseness, seams, level of constriction in certain areas (e.g. the shoulders) or labels sewn into them. Whatever the reason, it is important to understand that no one should have to feel discomfort to the point of distraction at best, pain at worst, simply by wearing clothes that are unsuited to them. Situations in which some kind of uniform is necessary (which includes formal and informal dress codes) are situations that might be assessed to identify whether a reasonable adjustment might be needed. This is already done in some instances for children – for example the wearing of a very specific school uniform – but I am less aware of it happening on a global scale for adults.

Just while I am on this point, I genuinely think that society would be far better off understanding that being comfortable in what one wears can be so beneficial – and yet we can be so judgemental and make so many assumptions based on appearance. Ways of presenting oneself in Western society can be seen as symbolic, from wearing a tie to the colour of clothes at a funeral. Much seems to be based on historical tradition, but all sorts of societal judgements are made – and sometimes, it should be ok to question these. If you are more productive at work wearing a t-shirt rather than a shirt and tie, and the reality is that it makes no discernible difference to the way you perform your role, then what is the problem? I am waiting for the day when I meet an academic professor in a full onesie and no one bats an eyelid.

Touch of animals

I have mentioned the smell of animals – the touch can be equally as sublime. Burying your face into a furry belly, or being laid on by a firm, heavy dog – these can be moments of magic. Never underestimate the sensorial power of the pet!

Texture of food

Some of you will enjoy food of a certain texture, and abhor food that falls outside of the requisite texture – this rarely has anything to do with taste, which many of the PNT find difficult to understand. But I believe that if you are texturally sensitive to food then the texture matters just as much, if not more, than whatever the food tastes like.

Hair and nails

While I have definitely written about this before it would be remiss of me not to do so again. You may experience the cutting of your hair and/or nails as painful. If so, there are some things that you might consider as alternatives. For example, the sensation of having wet hair or well-soaked nails differs to dry;

hair clippers differ from scissors. Filing nails more frequently than cutting them might be easier to bear. The environment in which these activities take place may also help – the more relaxed you are, the less likely it is that you will feel the pain. This is usually the area in which many of the PNT really struggle – how can it hurt to have one's hair cut? But there are enough first-hand narratives that tell us exactly that – so we simply have to take it into account.

Pain

Under-sensitivity and over-sensitivity in comparison with the PNT – and a combination thereof – is not an uncommon theme. Many of you will be able to tolerate a much higher level of pain than your PNT counterparts, while in other areas you may struggle. This is without doubt an area that requires more research – suffice to say that the processing of pain is very often qualitatively different. It goes without saying that having an awareness of how you are likely to process different kinds of pain is critical to your day-to-day living, and longer-term emotional state.

Along with pain, though a slightly differing area – and another one that requires some in-depth research – is how you might react to anaesthesia. As far as I know this is not a common issue, but I am very aware of some people who report that they do not respond to it in the same way, anaesthesia seemingly not having the impact it is supposed to do in the same way as for most people.

Taste

There are some areas relating to taste that you might be aware of, or need to be aware of in order to cater for your needs and reduce anxiety. In reality this is not always about taste, but eating in general – so I've grouped the areas together as it's all related to food!

Very bland or very strong

Many of you will have a strong preference for what others would identify as very bland food, or the other extreme of very spicy. I often wonder whether this is an actual preference as such, or whether it's a reflection of the sensitivity (or otherwise) of how you process taste. If, for example, you have an extreme sensitivity to taste then even the most bland food might be an explosion of taste for you. I guess there is no real way of knowing. But if you are one of those people who is constantly being harangued by others to try other food then it might be useful to point out that you are not being fussy, you just have super powerful taste buds!

May have limited diet – is that ok?

I am no health expert, but I hear so many stories from people who are accused of having 'too limited a diet'. It might be that you know what you enjoy, you have a routine of eating similar meals every day, and you stick to that routine. Sometimes when I ask what the actual meals are, they seem perfectly sound in terms of health and nutrition, and actually what the objection is from others is not that what you are eating is unhealthy, it just doesn't vary; in this instance I do have to wonder what the problem is. Of course there are many instances whereby a person's diet is restricted to the point of being seriously unhealthy, but that is a very different notion. In those cases I have known people to get around their limited diet by using supplements that are agreed by a health professional (e.g. additional vitamins) which have the effect of ensuring you are healthy without you having to compromise your eating habits.

The reality is that some limited diets really are perfectly ok; some limited diets might need additional supplements to ensure you are healthy; but some limited diets are a huge problem that require additional support. There seems to be a higher prevalence of apparent eating disorders within the adult population than within the PNT – so this is an area of concern. I do know some adults who have been diagnosed with an eating disorder and for whom symptomatically they fit the criteria; however, the restrictive diet (or similar) has actually been as a result of autistic anxiety and the need for control rather than areas that are sometimes more associated with eating disorders (such as body image). Of course, anyone can have an eating disorder – but for autistic adults it is sometimes the case that what appears to be an eating disorder is actually stemming from more autism-related issues. The section on global stability and balance will explore these issues in greater depth.

Tapas-style eating

Sometimes eating has more to do with how the food is presented, as opposed to how it tastes. I am a huge fan of buffet presentation, or tapas-style eating. In other words, where you have control over what you eat, how you eat it, what order you eat it in, and what I call 'food management'. If, for example, it provides sensory satisfaction to eat green on its own, then if you have the opportunity to choose green (let's say Thai green curry) in the first instance on its own, and only subsequently to eat white (the rice aspect), then hey presto, you get to eat a sensorily satisfying meal. If, on the other hand, some well-meaning soul delivers you a plate of exactly the same food but mixed together on the plate, then all of a sudden it might be intolerable. Food is a pretty important part of living in terms of health alone – it is also a pretty important part of life in terms of pleasure for many people too, so as much as can be done to suit your sensory needs, the better. Allowing for the opportunity for you to be in as much control as possible around food presentation could be invaluable for some.

Hating hearing/seeing others eat; hating eating in front of others

I have put these together – simply because the obvious solution is the same. Some of you will be adversely affected by having to eat within the vicinity of other people – this doesn't even need to be in the same room, it might be that if you can hear others eat (e.g. next door) then it is just as much an issue as if they were right next to you. There are any number of reasons why eating might be problematic for you when taking others into the equation, including:

- The noise of others' mastication: hearing others eat can be enough to put you off your food. If you are particularly sensitive to noise then there can be something deeply unpleasant about being forced to hear other people chewing.
- The smell of other people's food: it doesn't matter that they might even be eating the same food that has been prepared for

you, the invasiveness of the food on other people's plates can put you off your own food.

- The sight of people eating: they may be the most polite people in the universe – but even having to glimpse someone else eating while you are trying to tuck in yourself might be too much to process if you are going to enjoy your food.

- The intense discomfort at feeling others watching you eat: I think that this is one that is often ignored; some of you (and this might apply elsewhere in life) will be intensely uncomfortable with 'being in the spotlight' – irrespective of whether you actually are the centre of attention or not. For those of you who do not have a problem with eating in front of others, just imagine the following scenario:

You are placed in a circular room, right in the centre, with a small table and chair, and plate of food that you usually find delectable. However, there is a circle of chairs surrounding you, in close proximity, each of them homing a stranger to you. You are told that you have to eat every last mouthful before you are allowed to leave the room. As soon as you start to eat, those around you begin a running commentary all directly relating to you and your eating.

Rhetorical questions: does this make you uncomfortable? Does this make your eating experience less enjoyable than it would ordinarily be? If, given the chance, would you choose to eat on your own?

Now imagine that this is how you feel every single time you are encouraged to eat in front of other people.

- The necessity to converse: many of you may not have an issue with eating with others, so long as they don't expect you to be quite as chatty as they seem to want to be. It may be fine for them to keep up a running commentary of whatever they have in mind at the time – but if they expect you to join in, then there may be problems!

So many people that I know thoroughly enjoy food – preparing it (including for others), and eating it – and so many enjoy it as a solitary activity. However, I also know of so many of you who are essentially forced into not having that enjoyment simply because you are expected to eat with others. As noted later in the book, balance is key. Maybe there could be some level of compromise, in which you agree with other parties what balance is satisfactory for all, so that you are left in peace to enjoy meals but also agree to eat with them at certain times to fulfill their 'need' for eating as a social activity. Far be it for me to dictate what that balance might be – each to their own! But what I do implore those of you who don't have an issue with eating with others to understand is that being forced into such a situation over and over again, on a constant day-to-day basis, can seriously negatively impact wellbeing – it really is as important as that to take into account.

Preference for certain plates/bowls/cutlery

Some of you may happily scoff down all sorts of meals – so long as they are proffered on the appropriate receptacle, with the appropriate accompanying tools. Many folk simply don't realize the impact that what you eat from/off can play a huge part in the resulting experience – from having a thoroughly enjoyable meal to having to eat in misery.

Vestibular

Vestibular is all about movement, and the use of your inner ear system for balance (this is an extreme synopsis of course!). Many of you might have hyper- or hypovestibular sensory systems that need to be taken into account when understanding your sensory profile. For those of you who have hypersensitive vestibular systems, actions such as using an escalator, using ramps and going up and down stairs might cause feelings of imbalance or vertigo. My experience suggests that it is more common for you to have a love of movement, though, rather than a fear of it – which leads to:

- Stimming
- The need for movement
- The need to access equipment.

Stimming

Stimming might be conscious or subconscious, and is part and parcel of who you are. Sometimes you will hear people suggesting that stimming should be stopped or avoided or 'managed', but it is never quite as simple as that. It all comes down to why you are stimming, and whether it is causing an actual problem (as opposed to a perceived problem). For many of you, stimming should simply be a part of every day life that should be accepted by society, so long as it is not harmful or negatively disrupting. Hand flapping and the like can be borne out of excitement or anxiety – either way it is an expression of who you are. My view is that any stimming that cannot be categorized as harmful should be accepted within society as a means of expression; often, though, there seems to be a knee-jerk reaction that stimming should not be a part of public life – and yet there is often no logical rationale behind this. Pretty much everyone stims – the difference between you and the PNT is that you are likely to stim in a different way, and quite possibly more frequently and for longer periods of time. As with so much of what is written about in the book, if we had a society that better understood and accepted you for who you are, issues such as simple hand-flapping or stim-dancing would cease to be a problem – because so often the problem is not with the stim itself, it's with other people's reaction to it.

The need for movement

Some of you may thoroughly enjoy movements of the whole body, such as rocking or twirling. If your vestibular system craves such movement, often rhythmical in nature, then you shouldn't be forced into a position not to listen to it! It's your system's way of making sure that you feel physically satisfied and in control. No one likes the feeling of being physically out of control of your own body – so if you need to move in particular ways as a direct result of engaging in movement, then seeking to do so in ways that suit you is a must. Many of you may have discovered ways of doing this in engaging in activities such as martial arts or trampolining; some of you may be perfectly happy having a good rock when you get the chance and it's not an issue for anyone else. But to ignore this need is to increase anxiety! So, you might need . . .

Access to equipment

If you are a movement seeker, then it might be that certain types of equipment are the answer to your dreams. A hammock in the garden could mean the difference between stress and relaxation. Time and space in the office to access the trampette for a mini bounce could mean the difference between successful employment and disaster. Going on the see-saw with your partner could aid your relationship – and so on.

Proprioception

Proprioception relates to body awareness, both your own and how yours relates in the physical environment to what is around you. If your proprioceptive sensory system has a different profile compared to the PNT, then it will almost definitely be useful for you to find out. Some of the aspects of proprioception that might impact on you include:

- **Body awareness**: Some of you may be less aware of your body than others and might need measures to ensure that you are not constantly bumping into things or other people. Proprioception is closely liked with dyspraxia, so some of you may benefit from ascertaining whether you fit the criteria for dyspraxia and subsequently understand your proprioceptive capabilities in a more informed way. Even being aware of how proprioception impacts on you at a conscious level is likely to help – if, for example, you are consciously aware that your body doesn't automatically register what type of surface you are walking on, then it will increase the likelihood of you keeping an eye on the terrain.
- **Fine motor coordination – handwriting**: This is one that I continually try to promote as best as I can – the fact that some of you will find fine motor coordination significantly more problematic than others, and this can impact on handwriting – both time taken on it and legibility. I am firmly convinced that no one who has issues in this area should be forced to hand write unless it is absolutely necessary to do so; otherwise I fear that we would be heading into the domain of discrimination. If you need to take much longer to produce writing that is less

legible as a direct result of proprioceptive functioning, then surely it would be discriminatory not to allow you to use a laptop (or similar) if the circumstances allow.

- **Walking in a straight line:** As above, even being aware of this can be of great benefit. If you are aware that walking down a path with someone by your side traditionally ends up with you constantly tripping them over as you veer into their line of direction, you are more likely to make compensation to alleviate the issue.

Synaesthesia

If you are a synaesthete then you will process one type of sensory stimulation as if it were another. This might just be in one area, or there might be multiple areas that affect you. I think it must be incredibly difficult to know whether one is a synesthete, in a similar way as to how often people who are colour blind won't find out for years that this is the case. Much of it will be based on a chance comment or encounter, I suspect. However, being armed with the knowledge that such a sensory phenomenon might apply to you gives you the chance to investigate it.

Interoception

Interoception involves being aware of internal sensations that could include:

Feeling hungry/full/the need to go to the toilet

Some of you may not know what feeling hungry feels like, and/or what feeling full feels like. The issues associated with this are obvious – you may well under eat, over eat, or find yourself in a confusing situation that both are eminently possible on any given day. It is essential for your health to identify whether your interoception allows you to feel hunger or satiation; if not, then clearly planned meals are probably the way forward for you. Similarly, if there is an explanation as to why your body sometimes doesn't reveal to you when you need to go to the toilet, it can do wonders for your self-esteem.

Awareness of organs – heartbeat, respiration

Some of you may be less aware of internal organs than most – for example not being aware of your heartbeat, whether it is beating faster than usual, or whether your breathing patterns have changed.

Links between interoception and emotional awareness and regulation

There are links between interoception and emotional awareness and regulation – which demonstrates just how useful it might be to ascertain how your proprioception works for you. There is much that we need to learn about interoception, but it is an emerging field with some narratives around how you might go about working with your body to improve your interoception, if that is what is needed.

Just because something works in one context doesn't mean it works across the board

Just a last note on this sensory section – please don't ever fall into the trap of making the assumption that what works in one scenario automatically works in another. No two environments are the same! Some common mistakes that I have come across that include this issue, along with some others, are as follows:

- The assumption that if you can have an enjoyable time in a crowded environment (e.g. a music gig) then this automatically means that you cannot have an issue with other crowded situations (e.g. using a lift at a busy time).
- That if you are ok with one level of noise then all levels of noise, irrespective of what the source of the noise is, are also acceptable.
- That if you can 'cope' with one sensory situation one day then that will always be the case.
- That sensory needs are preferences, as opposed to actual needs.
- That if you just 'tried harder' then your sensory system will listen and somehow respond.
- That your sensory preferences are deliberately created to annoy the rest of the world – this is such a frustrating one! The idea

that you need to stim, or sit in the office with no shoes on, is as a result of you wanting to deliberately annoy others is so nonsensical, and yet it is often the reaction that you will encounter.

- That if you are 'allowed' sensory adjustments then every other person in the vicinity will immediately want them as well – why, oh why do people make this assumption? The reality is that unless others actually need sensory adjustments, then they won't want them; and if they do need them, great – you've made another reasonable adjustment!
- That your sensory needs are made up – why on earth would anyone make up a sensory profile that doesn't apply to their self?
- That you will 'grow out of it' – yes, sensory profiles can change over time (and many will) but it is not a valid assumption to make for all of you.

4
Access to GP/hospital/dentist/healthcare

It is clear that you are of a population for whom there are additional difficulties in accessing provision that should be available to everyone, in an equal way, whenever possible. In an area that is of such importance as healthcare we simply must do better to meet your needs. This chapter aims to identify some of the possible reasons why you might not access healthcare in the same way as the PNT, puts forward some individual accounts of what might constitute the 'dream appointment', and finally identifies some tips for health institutions that they could adopt if they are aiming to reduce your anxiety as much as possible. The latter should be done in a general proactive way; but it would also be highly relevant to identify what your individual needs are in case additional changes are required.

As with most things within the autism world, the fault is absolutely not to be laid at your feet. We are a far cry from providing the support you need to access healthcare on an equal footing compared to most other people. There may be reasons for not accessing healthcare that relate to being autistic, but if we had a system that actually met your needs then my belief is that this risk would either reduce or be neutralized – in which case one could conclude that it isn't being autistic that precludes you from access, it is the systems themselves.

You may well be aware of things such as hospital passports which are meant to act as a way of identifying what your needs are; these can be fantastic, but as there are still ongoing issues with accessing healthcare on a wide scale, we still have more to do.

What the issues are

There are some reasons that might influence you not accessing healthcare in the first place. These include:

- **Not knowing that you need to go**: If you are the sort of individual who struggles with identifying your own health needs, then it might be that you either don't access health care when you need to, or have stopped accessing healthcare because you've tried to in the past only to be told that there is no issue. Either way, it is likely in this scenario that you will be more at risk of a health condition remaining untreated compared to others. If this is the case then it is very wise indeed to develop a system with all relevant healthcare facilities to have check ups as frequently as is required, and on a regular basis. I see no reason why this could not be presented as a reasonable adjustment.

- **Making yourself accept that you need to go**: Many of you may have issues with self-esteem and self-worth; this might lead you to thinking that you are not worthy of accessing healthcare, or that you should not be what you perceive as a burden to others. What I like to point out in such circumstances is that first off you are, of course, equal as a human to any other person – but also that these healthcare professionals would be out of a job if no one accessed their services!

- **Not being registered**: The administration of life might be something that you really struggle with. If you've moved house or, for whatever reason, are not registered with the GP or dentist then, even when you feel ill, you may simply decide that it is easier to put up with the illness rather than having to go through the process of getting yourself registered. I have also known people who feel as though they are almost 'cheating the system' by registering for services and then immediately requesting an appointment.

The reality is that the vast majority of health facilities provide for a huge range of individuals, and will not be worried in the slightest if you need to register and then immediately ask to be seen. However, for your own peace of mind, it is well worth considering taking the time to draw up a list of all the potential health facilities you should be registered with, and get support to get registered. This might be an advocacy service, a family member, or someone you might be able to pay for if you have financial support for independent living; the main thing is to get registered so that when the time comes it is one less thing to get anxious about.

Knowledge that the professional may not understand you, or believe you

This is such a common issue in my experience. So many of you will believe that the professional either won't understand what your needs are, or that they will not even believe what you are actually saying. This could be because of past experiences, or it may be that you have a sensory need that is so far off the radar for the professional that they struggle to either understand or believe you. I don't know of a quick fix for this – unless you wanted to show them a copy of this section of the book! Whatever the reason, your health is important enough for you to be taken seriously. Remember that you will often have the right to seek a second opinion. It might also be useful to have someone who can advocate on your behalf to be with you to help explain your unique position. This might not only assist in getting your points across, it might help alleviate anxiety of you having to attend the appointment.

Making an appointment

Systems that are often in place for healthcare settings may not be the most autism-friendly in the universe. Many of them use a phone system without many or any alternatives, although GP surgeries are getting a lot better at using electronic booking systems. The reality is, though, if you find using a phone problematic to the point of preferring to put up with that awful toothache rather than having to face the ordeal of ringing the dentist, then you are at a significant disadvantage. Rather than waiting until you have an actual problem, it might be worth engaging with the practice to explain what the issue is and to ascertain what alternatives they can offer you for when a situation arises.

The terror of last time

It can be difficult to get over the experience of a traumatic visit to the doctor (or whichever profession that relates to you) and the ongoing anxiety can be very difficult to overcome. However, it is well worth training yourself to remember that all experiences are different, and there are certain things that you have in your control to try and alleviate the risk of the past repeating itself. Following a traumatic event, it might be beneficial to note down exactly what it was that caused the issue – in this way it becomes somewhat objectified, and possibly easier to work out which aspects of the experience you may be able to influence in the future. For example, if the stress was as a result of the GP waiting room being full, and your appointment was delayed by half an hour, then contacting the surgery to request that you have the very first appointment of the day should go some way towards taking that risk out of the equation.

Being alone

I am a great believer in advocacy support, so if you have anyone in your life that you trust to accompany you on a visit, then make use of them. It might be that they can be briefed on any issues you have so that they can be a spokesperson – they can also be an incredibly useful resource for reminding you what was actually said during the appointment – sometimes it might be that you are so stressed that not a lot of the information provided is retained. If you don't have someone to go with you and you find that you don't recall information readily, then asking to record the appointment using an audio device could be an option. You would need to check with the individual/s in question first, though.

Fear of the unknown

The problem with no two experiences being the same means that there will always be a sense of the unknown for any healthcare appointment. But it might be that there are some things that you can find out for yourself that reduce the unknown factors involved. Having a specific named person who will be seeing you, making sure that the surgery knows that you cannot be expected to be asked for a student to be present at the start of the appointment, being familiar with the environment – these are the sorts of things that you might be able to organize so that there is a reduced chance of heading into an appointment with no concrete aspects to rely on.

Fear of the outcome

One of your biggest fears might be that you are worried about what the outcome might be. This is common across many populations – but the reality is that whatever might be wrong, *is already wrong* – the appointment is to find out what this actually is and begin whatever road to recovery that might be possible. So many people are reluctant to find out if there is anything wrong with them, when in fact the actual appointment is merely an information gathering exercise; not going will not stop the problem occurring – if there is a problem then it has already occurred. In some way, readjusting your parameters to realizing that going to your appointment is the first step to getting a problem solved, rather than an end point of finding out what the problem is, can be very affirming indeed.

What can healthcare do?

I am not suggesting that all of the following suggestions are legally binding, but I do think that all healthcare providers could, at least, consider whether there might be a way forward to reduce risk of being discriminatory. In this section my narrative is aimed at those healthcare settings, rather than you as the autistic reader.

Tips for accessing healthcare settings

- Immediate request for communication preferences
- Multiple options for making an appointment
- Option of home visits
- Option of appointment outside of usual hours
- Offer of advocacy – do you want someone else present?
- Video footage of the area
- Appointment time offer
- Online engagement if possible
- One-way system
- No need to queue at reception
- Named personnel of who will be present

- Information gathering prior to appointment
- As much detail as possible of how the appointment will run and timings
- Links to video clips identifying similar treatments that the patient can expect
- Sensory questionnaire to identify potential sensory issues that can be taken into consideration.

Immediate request for communication preferences

This tip could be expanded to pretty much any organization! As soon as an autism identification is disclosed, seek what the person's communication preferences are. Identify pertinent communication information. Here is a framework that you might want to consider – and adapt to suit your own setting:

List the following in order of preference:

- Phone
- Email
- Text
- Video call
- Face-to-face
- Alternative messenger service.

Are there any forms of communication that are too anxiety-inducing for you to engage with?

If we need to contact you, would you prefer for us to text first to let you know what time it is likely to be, and in what format?

If we need to ask you questions, would you prefer a list of those questions in advance – if so, how long in advance would be best?

Multiple options for making an appointment

There may be technical issues with this, but the more options an autistic person has in terms of how they might make an appointment, the better. It is not unusual for an autistic adult to find it distressing to use the phone so, if a phone-only system is the only option, it could be seen as discriminatory if there are other options that could be utilized.

Option for home visits

Home visits are common in some professions – and yet, in others, there seems to be a blanket policy of never considering them. Why this is the case is something that I don't readily understand. If a person, for example, is in need of support, but their anxiety precludes them from leaving the house, then surely a home visit is something that should be considered, otherwise might that person miss out on vital healthcare?

Option of an appointment outside of usual hours

Many autistic adults would prefer appointments at certain times that better suit them – not least at times where it is much less likely that they will have to mix with other people. Having autism-friendly slots, for example in the evening, once a week, might make the difference between an autistic person accessing the provision, or not.

Offer of advocacy – do you want someone else present?

Unless there are reasons whereby an advocate cannot be used, make it clear that you welcome others to attend the appointment alongside the autistic person. Making this option available as a matter of course both allows the autistic person to consider it if they had not done so before, or relieves the autistic person of going through the anxiety of having to request it.

Video footage of the area

Simple, but effective – having a video clip of what the building looks like, and doing a 'walk-through' so that the watcher is able to 'see' what they will experience can help alleviate anxiety, is pretty much cost free, and, as with many of these suggestions, increases the possibility of the autistic person having trust that you have some understanding of autism.

Appointment time offer

If it is not possible to have almost bespoke options, it might be possible to at least ensure that there are appointments that are kept free which are at the very start of the working day. This has the benefit of a reduction of risk of waiting times, and reduction of risk of having to meet other people. Ideally, if you were to offer (for example) an 8.30am appointment, the person should be able to go straight through to meet with the professional without having to engage with anyone else at all.

Online engagement if possible

Consider the option of having an appointment online. This is getting more and more popular, and is well worth investigating. Many autistic people will feel almost infinitely more comfortable when in a familiar, trusted, environment – so offering this option may again mean the difference between a person being treated – or not.

One-way system

As noted, some autistic people will struggle if there is an increased need for interaction. Having a fully one-way system from entrance to waiting room (if you really need a waiting room) to appointment to exit that is clearly labelled would help alleviate that risk.

No need to queue at reception

Queuing in general often poses a problem for autistic individuals; doing so at a time in which anxiety levels are likely to be high anyway could just make matters worse. Self-check-in options are getting more prevalent – but are by no means widespread among all providers. Having the clear option to either check in using a self-service option, or to have a face-to-face option would be preferable to just having one or the other.

Named personnel of who will be present

Prior to the appointment, make sure that the individual knows exactly who they will be meeting with.

Information gathering prior to appointment

Some appointments require a question-and-answer type session at the start; as with many communicative situations, this could cause unnecessary anxiety for an autistic person if the same information could have been gathered and shared well before the appointment. It also has the added benefit of reducing the duration of the appointment – this makes it more efficient, but often also less stressful for the individual.

As much detail as possible of how the appointment will run and timings

This is obviously not always easy to do, and you would not want to provide misleading information. So, this suggested tip may not be appropriate for all provision at all times. However, if it is possible to give information on what the process will be, and likely timings (e.g. what to expect from beginning to end for an MRI scan), it will likely be useful information for the autistic person accessing the service.

Links to video clips identifying similar treatments that the patient can expect

There are so many video clips online, it might be relatively easy for you to identify some (or even create your own) to demonstrate what a procedure will look like. For example, if someone has made an appointment to have their blood pressure taken, it should be simple to give links to a similar procedure so that there is an understanding as to what to expect.

Sensory questionnaire to identify potential sensory issues that can be taken into consideration

It would be so useful for all provision to have a sensory 'checklist' or questionnaire to identify whether there is anything that can be done to alleviate 'sensory anxiety'.

The autism-specific healthcare complex

In addition to these points that individual practices could develop, my absolute dream of an autism-friendly system would be to have autism-specific healthcare facilities that are accessible to all of you in one place, staffed by specialists not just in their field of health, but in the field of autism. Rather than having to rely on an individual GP within a surgery to have an understanding of your autistic needs, all staff within the autism-specific healthcare complex would be 'qualified' in terms of their autism understanding. In other words, an autism-specific qualification that had approval from the autistic population would be necessary for all staff who work there. Not only could this massively decrease healthcare-related anxiety for you, and, presumably, massively improve your wellbeing (physical, mental, and emotional) but it could also be a very cost-effective way of meeting need.

Included in the complex, which would be sized dependent on the population, would be all the healthcare professionals that a person might need to access over a lifetime – GPs, dentists, podiatrists, physiotherapists, occupational therapists, speech and language therapists, mental health professionals, etc. Every single one of them would be qualified in a suitable autism-specific qualification (my preference would be at Masters level), as would all other staff involved in direct communication with you – for example the receptionist. It would literally be a 'one-stop shop' for all your healthcare needs, and if run properly would be the safe haven for all adults within that area to access what is rightfully theirs to access. While this might sound like an irresponsible suggestion that will never be reality, I believe that it is, in fact, what we need to be aspiring to.

The cost benefit from a financial perspective is that all the reasonable adjustments that could be made are all of a sudden being made for the majority population, not the minority. If we understand that the prevalence of autism is between 1–2 per cent, then in general practice that is between one and two people per hundred accessing a provision who are autistic. It might be difficult for that provision to justify, for example, the costs involved in changing the sensory environment to make it more autism-friendly. If, on the other hand, your provision caters for a population of whom 100 per cent are autistic – then it might make perfect sense. This goes right across the board – it may be difficult putting forward the idea of getting staff 'autism-qualified' when so few people you engage with are autistic in mainstream provision, but for an autism-specific provision it would make absolute sense.

Benefits might include:

- **Each professional has their own case load**: If each professional had their own case load they would become familiar with you on an individual basis. No longer would you have to explain to yet another GP what you have explained a dozen times before, as they would already know you. No longer would you have to face the fear of meeting yet another healthcare professional for the first time. No longer would you have to establish what your preferred communication style might be. The list could go on – but having a professional who is a specialist three times over – in their profession, in autism, and in you – could surely only be a good thing.

- **Cradle to grave**: So many services are divided between children and adults – there are some very good reasons for this, but for many of you this means having to explain things all over again. GPs are not bound by this age restriction and this has its own benefits. It might be that the child/adult cut off has to stay in place within certain professions, but at least if those services reside within the same complex – so that those groups of individuals can provide seamless transitions – then the disruption so often found will reduce.

- **Cost-effective way of making reasonable adjustments**: It might not be considered 'reasonable' for a whole mainstream dentist surgery to have soundproof walls to assist with one person's sensory needs – but if the entire patient population is autistic then all of a sudden many sensory and other adjustments could be undertaken. This seems to me to be a very cost-effective way to providing equality for you as a population, with the ultimate aim of genuine accessibility.

The most obvious benefit of all is that we would be striving towards healthy autistic adults, rather than accepting the frightening reality that we currently live with.

I wrote this chapter without being aware of the work done by Mary Doherty, 'The Autistic Doctor', on barriers to healthcare for autistic adults. I have since been very interested to read her papers, and some references to further reading can be found at the end of the book.

5

Diagnosis/identification

I am categorically not a clinician, so I am not able to comment on some aspects of the diagnostic process – however, this chapter will go through some thoughts on the whole process based on what I have learned over the years. I accept that others will have differing opinions, particularly on the whole debate around how we should be conceptualizing autism – this is just my perspective, which I aim to tie in with the whole theme of anxiety.

The current terminology that most of you will be aware of is diagnosis. Some of you will have a diagnosis of Asperger Syndrome (AS), and some of you will have a different diagnosis, for example, Autistic Spectrum Disorder. While AS is no longer in the diagnostic manual that is commonly used (the *Diagnostic Manual for Psychiatric Disorders*, fifth edition – DSM-5, 2013), there is clear guidance that the label is still absolutely valid, as many of you will have been 'diagnosed' prior to the changes in the DSM. You will note that I put 'diagnosis' here in inverted commas – the reason for this is that I don't believe that it is an appropriate term for discovering who you are. My belief is that autism is not a disorder, or a medical illness or 'condition', but a different way of processing information. The attempt at my definition in a previous book is as follows:

> Autism refers to a neurotype that leads to a cognition that is quali-tatively different from that of the PNT in the way that information specific to communication, social interpretation and interaction is processed and understood; and to a perceptual reality of the sensory environment that differs considerably from one individual to the next.

As you can see, there is no negative, medical-based deficit-orien-tated language within this definition. The notion of a 'diagnosis' is that we are diagnosed with something that is wrong with us, and that we are seeking to fix it somehow – alleviate the symptoms, or cure ourselves of whatever we are diagnosed with. I strongly feel that this is vastly inappropriate when it comes to autism. We don't, presumably, want to 'fix' being autistic – there is no 'fix' as autism is a part of who you are. The notion that you are somehow in need of fixing is, in fact, one of the most intrinsic reasons behind common anxiety. After all, how easy is it to live an existence in which you are always required to be different to whom you inherently are? It's a no-win situation. If we all accepted autism as a way of being, not a *lesser* way of being, then perhaps this would go a long way towards alleviating daily stress. How about this as the seventh reasonable adjustment:

> *Autistic people are not seen within the context of being lesser; in other words, they were accepted for who they are and their natural way of being, as opposed to some kind of deficit-riddled human that is in need of fixing.*

I am not suggesting for one moment that we don't provide the support that some of you may require, or do everything we can to alleviate the extreme distress that you might find yourself in – but this is not about changing your autism as such, it's about working out what combination of factors has led to the distress and changing those. The key here is to understand that being autistic is not the problem in and of itself. The sooner we realize that not all autistic people live problematic lives, the better. Some people believe that you can't really be autistic *unless* your life is a problem. I categorically refute this notion. I am a firm believer that being autistic within the wrong environment is usually problematic, on a sliding scale from being at a mild disadvantage to absolutely catastrophic – with every possible state in between. And you may well move along that sliding scale, sometimes on a minute-to-minute basis, sometimes over a period of years. The point, then, is that logically if you can move along that scale, and you can't change being autistic, then other factors must be at play. In addition, if you are autistic and are in the *right* environment, then you will not be in a problematic state.

So, the notion that you somehow have to be negatively impacted to be 'allowed' to be autistic seems hugely contradictory.

Another way of putting it is thus: we do not seem to be able to agree on many things that are related to autism; one thing, however, that we do pretty much all agree on is that being autistic is from birth to death. You are born autistic, and you will continue to be autistic. What, then, about the child who neatly fits the current descriptions of autism that relate to being negatively impacted by autism – but circumstances change so that by the time the child is an adult, she is partnered with the person who is an ideal 'fit', is self-employed doing the work that she is passionately interested in, and lives in a smallholding of nine acres so that, in her spare time, she can ride her beloved horse. There are literally no negative days for her in relation to being autistic – but she is just as autistic as she was when she was a child. A similar example – and this is one I have witnessed on a number of occasions – is the individual who has all sorts of day-to-day problems – until he moves abroad. The stories from individuals who have made such a move have a common theme – back 'home' (i.e. prior to the move) they were looked down upon, and struggled in many areas. But as a person who is not native to the country/culture/language/systems/custom etc. they are instantly 'forgiven' for the way that they are and accepted simply as someone who does not 'naturally fit in'. If such acceptance for a 'different way of being' is possible – which it clearly is for those individuals – why are we not striving for a similar level of acceptance within society as a whole? I should point out here that moving abroad will not be the solution for all of you! It was merely an example of real-life experiences to make a point.

So – I am not a fan of 'diagnosis' or words associated with the current process, such as 'impairment', 'disorder' and 'deficit' (among others). I am a fan, however, of the notion of 'identification'. Being identified as autistic could mean that you go through a similar process but just with a differing term – which might change the whole dynamic at a conceptual level. Conceptualizing yourself as having an identity that is more apt to you than the PNT, as opposed to getting a diagnosis of something problematic, may change the way in which you understand yourself.

The pros of diagnosis

The discussion here relates to anxiety, as I have written elsewhere around autism identification in adults. There are also other aspects that might be useful, for example having a better understanding of what your rights are under The Equality Act, which I will touch on later. In relation, then, to anxiety the pros include:

- Validity of self
- Apportioning blame
- Having a better truth
- Providing armour against the world
- Understanding identity
- Looking to the future.

Validity of self

It might be that you have always felt an outsider – the number of people I know who reflect on the fact that they have always felt a little bit different (or a lot different, sometimes) but never knew why. Being identified gives you that validity of self, of who you are, and allows you to realize that you were, in fact, right all along!

Apportioning blame

In relation to anxiety, this is huge. It might be that others have had a history of blaming you as an individual for things that you struggle with, or things that you have been deemed to have been in the wrong about. But understanding those past events through a different lens – in other words seeing yourself as a perfectly functioning autistic as opposed to a broken PNT – means that you may no longer have to accept that blame. Being anxious about being in the 'wrong', sometimes perpetually, is a tough state to be in. But by understanding that you are not always in the wrong, you are a product of being autistic in a PNT environment that is judging you incorrectly, can do wonders for accepting that you should not always be blamed for being who you are.

Having a better truth

I love this concept of you understanding yourself within the context of truth; it is similar to the points that I have already made – but there is definitely a peace to be found when you are given the opportunity to find out what truths apply to you – and, just as importantly, what other people's perceived truths could be rejected. Understanding that you are not lazy, or incompetent, or academically poor, as opposed to a closer truth that you have simply been judged within a PNT context that doesn't work for you, can be illuminating and assist in reducing stress to a massive degree.

Providing armour against the world

Knowledge of your own identity is critical if you are going to successfully navigate society without undue anxiety. Knowing your own strengths and weaknesses within your autism context will likely reduce risk of you making decisions that risk anxiety. In this sense, autism knowledge is powerful indeed.

Understanding identity

I will be writing about this in more detail later, but it is worth thinking about in the context of whether or not you are deciding on getting formally identified as autistic. Some of you may feel that you need that formal identification in order to move forward. Some of you may be content 'knowing yourself' without it being formally recognized (by which I mean the 'diagnosis'). Either way, having that understanding of your own identity will likely help reduce anxiety in the long run.

Looking to the future

It is with no hesitation that I suggest that having the knowledge of your own identity, for almost all of you, will be useful in terms of understanding of self and looking to the future. To constantly strive to be a PNT when you are autistic is highly likely to be exhausting and anxiety-ridden. To have the secure knowledge that you are autistic, though, should help plan goals, and get rid of aims that on reflection are not particularly suitable for you.

The cons of diagnosis

The cons of being identified don't relate so much to you being autistic, they are more about other people's understanding of you, so in a sense you might not think they fit in this category in the strictest sense – perhaps they are more around clarifying what you might expect so that it can help with decision making:

Getting identified will not solve all your problems

It seems to be a common theme that when you realize that you are autistic, there can be almost a period of euphoria, when so many things all of a sudden fall into place. This might not be the case, of course, so don't worry if you don't fit this pattern. However, there might also be a period of time that is much harder to live through, when you realize that even though you now have a better understanding of who you are, it won't necessarily or automatically make your life instantly better. It *might* make your life instantly better – but this is by no means a guarantee. Change (of anxiety states, for example) is likely to be a longer-term goal, rather than an instant fix.

Other people might change their attitude towards you

Other people might actually perceive you as a different person after you have shared with them that you are autistic. Why this is the case is beyond me. I have heard stories of decades old friends who have suddenly no longer wanted contact, or family members changing their attitude, just based on the identification. Perhaps this is because they don't actually believe that you are autistic, and resent the fact that you now have that identity – this is sometimes the case, and is usually as a result of the person not having a very good understanding of autism in the first place. Whatever the reason, this kind of reaction can be extremely upsetting.

Assumptions that are inaccurate

I mention this in the very first chapter, but it is worth reiterating. So many people will have preconceptions as to what autism means to them, and then apply those assumptions to you. They are very likely, just from a statistical probability position, not to be accurate.

My view, for what it's worth, is that in a general sense it is almost always worth understanding your autistic identity – but that you should be very careful to whom you disclose this identity. This relates directly to asking yourself the question, 'Will this increase or decrease anxiety for whatever reason?' It might be useful to take all of the above (and what has been written elsewhere) into account before deciding on the disclosure issue. But do remember – once you have disclosed, there is no taking it back!

One additional issue around disclosure is that you should consider the impact on anxiety around some of the more common things you might hear people saying, and whether these things are aimed at you on a personal level. My belief is that it is less stressful to hear people's inaccurate views on autism at an objective level; if those views are directed at you as they know you are autistic then the impact might be greater. Sometimes a good compromise is to disclose to those who you feel either might know (or suspect) anyway, and/or who might be absolutely accepting at the very least, or even massively supportive in the long term. Disclosure to those individuals can be such a lovely and affirming experience – being able to honestly be your true self in their company, for example, can do wonders to balance out the stress of not necessarily being able to do so elsewhere.

Lastly, it would be remiss of me not to mention the very small minority of people for whom an autism identity might be a particularly negative experience. These include:

- **Those who already have a very rigid and negative perspective of what autism is.** If someone has a very negative view of autism – for whatever reason – and is also the sort of person who has very rigid and strong beliefs in general, it is likely that they will not be persuaded to change. It might be that they know an autistic person and feel that they are nothing like them, so would reject the notion completely, or have a stereotypical view of autism as learned from society and again refuse to accept the identity themselves.

- **Those who are elderly and for whom the realization at such a late stage might be too much of a shock.** Sadly, identification services have always 'missed' people who are autistic. It is very likely that there are generations of autistics, many of whom have been missed. Some of those might be at a stage in life whereby a complete and (sometimes) dramatic change in how they perceive themselves – however accurate that might be – could be anxiety-inducing in its own right. This is absolutely not to suggest that age is directly correlated with whether to seek an identification (or to suggest it to someone else), but logic dictates that the longer you live without the knowledge, the greater the risk of that new knowledge being more of a shock. I do also happen to know people in their retirement years being identified with great success.

- **Those for whom knowing how things might have been different is a trauma in itself.** Sometimes it can be extremely difficult to reflect on 'what might have been' – if the identification had been sooner. This should also be taken into account when working out whether to broach the subject (either with self or others) as it could be a negative spiral if you are the sort of person who cannot bear to think how different life might have been if you had been identified at a younger age, or before a significant event in your life. The whole point of this book is to avoid anxiety for autistic adults – and for a small number of people it must be recognized that in order to avoid anxiety, an autism identification might also need to be avoided – which is ironic indeed. It should be noted, though, that the vast majority of people I am aware of who are identified in adulthood, are very pleased that they have got their autism identification.

Waiting time

There are probably a whole host of issues with the current identification provision, not least that it is currently very 'post coded' – in other words what you will expect to get in terms of support in one region is likely to differ, sometimes quite considerably, to another. However, one thing that is very often reported by adults is that they had to go on to a lengthy waiting list before they were 'assessed' – and these waiting lists are not uncommonly counted in years, rather than months. This can be excruciatingly anxiety-inducing for some of you, which is why I feel that it is important to note. This is just food for thought – but does make a potentially extremely important point, which is . . .

If being anxious puts you at a significant disadvantage – and if you are the sort of person who will be in a state of extreme anxiety once your referral has been made – and if the waiting time is lengthy . . . how does that 'fit' with The Equality Act? In other words – and this is the crucial bit – would a reduction of waiting times for that population be deemed a reasonable adjustment? If so, then could *not* making every effort to reduce waiting times be considered discriminatory?

My ideas for future identification services, in other words some aspects I think we could strive towards with the idea of reducing anxiety, include:

- Self-referral options
- All clinicians highly qualified in autism
- Removal of traditional bricks and mortar assessment centres
- Diagnostic terminology to be reconsidered
- Flexible options of when to go through the identification process
- Flexible options for the process itself, taking individuals, needs into account.

Self-referral options

As noted in Chapter 4, many of you will be reluctant to go to the GP. I feel that very often the need for a GP referral is just another barrier to pursuing your identification, and barriers should be made as minimal as possible. If you are autistic and you have a knowledgeable GP then you will be referred on – in which case why not 'allow' the autistic person to self-refer and remove that stage? Or you will have a GP who does not understand that you are autistic and therefore refuses to refer you – in which case you are denied the opportunity to be identified. Of course, there are other reasons why many services insist on a GP referral, such as having discussions around the pros and cons of an identification – my view is that the identification provision itself could provide most, if not all, of those services, from within a specialist setting.

All clinicians highly qualified in autism

Clinicians – by definition – are highly trained; however, this does not automatically mean that they have all had extensive autism training as part of their journey. Many disciplines pay little attention to autism over years of training; this is obviously not always the case, but there is an extreme inconsistency in what is provided in terms of autism understanding. I genuinely believe that such an important process (the autism identification) should be undertaken by those who have an additional autism qualification that is consistent across the board.

Removal of traditional bricks and mortar assessment centres

Many of you will have been required to attend an assessment in a very medically based environment; not only can this be intimidating, it might also lead to you having much higher anxiety than, for example, an area that you have some say in identifying. In the same way as in Chapter 4 on healthcare settings, I often wonder why you can't go through an identification process in the safety of your own home.

Diagnostic terminology to be reconsidered

These musings are my own, and not from a clinician – however, I do think that there are ways of framing autism accurately without having to revert to pejorative and possibly harmful terms. For example, I believe that 'Autistic Spectrum Disorder' could just as easily (and in my view way more accurately) be redefined as 'autism'. A revamp of the terms, taking autistic adults' views into account, could do much to decrease anxiety and even possibly increase societal understanding of autistic adults.

Flexible options of when to go through the identification process

Again, in line with Chapter 4 on healthcare, I feel that you should have more control over the timing of your identification. Going through the process can be highly anxiety-inducing in its own right, so the more than can be done to reduce or alleviate that anxiety the better. If that means that for some of you an evening would be far better than the morning or even, dare I say it, for those of you who may prefer a nocturnal existence, a night-time process could be accommodated.

Flexible options for the process itself, taking individuals' needs into account

Sometimes you will have been precluded from an assessment because of the rigidity of the assessment protocol. I do not think that this should ever be acceptable. Certainly none of the reasons that I am aware of should have been valid. For example, it might be preferable if the assessor is able to have a conversation with a parent in order to glean information from their perspective – and I have known people to be refused an assessment because no parent is available. Similarly, I have known individuals to be refused an assessment because they have asked to bring their partner with them. The list could go on – my view is that at this incredibly important time of your life, your needs should be taken into account so long as the integrity of the process is not compromised, and that the needs are not such that it is unreasonable to expect them to be met.

6

University

Not all of you will have gone to university (or will go to university), but there will be enough of you to warrant this chapter. This is, in part, because there are too many autistic university students who are still being failed by Higher Education in my view. If a student is forced to drop out of study at Further Education or Higher Education as a result of the environment being too anxiety-inducing, then my reasoning is that something is going wrong at the institutional level. This isn't to suggest that all institutions can cater for all autistic students, but I am sure that there is still work to do until we hit a stage that is satisfactory at the very least.

This chapter will identify just some of the areas of student life that you might find cause anxiety. The first 'half' of the chapter covers some of the things you might want to consider as part of your educational journey. The second 'half', in a sense, is for the educational institution to take into account to work on your behalf to reduce anxiety. I am by no means suggesting that every institution should meet all the 'targets' that I am putting forward as possible ways to reduce risk of discrimination – these are suggestions only. In a sense this is an optimistic view of a potential future where you are provided with as risk-free study as possible – so long as we are striving towards that, at least we can then ensure that we are working in the right direction.

I am not particularly distinguishing between Further Education and Higher Education – I will refer to 'education' from this point on for the sake of simplicity. Some aspects will cover both and are general points around study; some are more focused towards one or the other. Lastly, I make no mention of age – education can be lifelong; college life is not exclusive to young adults.

Applying to study

So – right from the outset you may be at a disadvantage! If the application process itself causes you anxiety because of the way in which you are required to fill forms in, then could this potentially be discriminatory as a route towards education? My view is that the less flexible the options are for pretty much any process of application, the higher the risk of not being able to take individual need into account. I would love the future to hold a system whereby there were different routes to applying to institutions that were flexible enough to take autistic cognitive styles into account. This will be a common theme throughout this chapter – diversity of processes, to me, are crucial in order to reduce anxiety and to meet need. Some might argue that at an institutional level there has to be a standardized method of application, otherwise the system itself is too unwieldy – but I am convinced that if there were fair and equitable ways of applying that differed in their presentation, the system would still be manageable. I will be expanding on this notion later in the chapter.

Choice

How to choose where to go to study can be a painful experience for many of you. It might be a useful way forward to list the priorities that you have for what you want out of the experience – in other words, what are the most important aspects of education to take into account. Doing this can enable a more objective way of identifying where to apply. Things that you could consider include (in no particular order):

- Type of accommodation on offer
- The course itself
- Duration of course
- Proximity to your current home
- What type of social life there might be within the locality
- Grades required for the course
- The way in which the course is taught
- The physical environment – where you are expected to access
- Whether the course is likely to lead to a vocational activity

- Where is the institution placed in league tables?
- Is the focus more on pure academia or more of an applied institution?
- Is there easy access to extra curricula activity that interests you?
- Is there a specific neurodiversity statement/movement/club within the institution/locality?
- What is the reputation for supporting autistic students?
- What types of assessments are used within the course?

Choosing which of the above is of importance to you, adding to the list, and subsequently putting them in order of priority might be a way of reducing anxiety over how to make such a difficult choice. It might be that there are certain stipulations that are 'make or break' – so, for example, if you are absolutely certain that you would not be able to access an institution that requires public transport (e.g. a course is taught on different campuses with buses running between them) in which case this will also help your decision making. The points below might also be beneficial to consider when making your choices over continued education.

Understanding the abstract

Anxiety is so often as a result of not having a clear understanding as to what to expect. In many cases you may have never had the opportunity to know what university life might be like. This is where forward planning could be crucial. If there are opportunities for you to visit students (e.g. a sibling) then it could be a very beneficial experience to do so. Even then, though, while you may get some glimpse into student life, it won't be the exact same as what your own experiences are likely to be. Having some level of focus will help – so, for example, knowing which institution you wish to apply for and visiting that specific city, accessing open days, reading up on a specific course – these are all possible options that could de-mystify the abstract notion of what the future holds.

Accommodation

This might be one of the most important aspects of student life for some of you. Having to live with others who cause direct anxiety can be a miserable experience; not knowing whom you could end up living with could also be a massive source of anxiety itself. And yet it might be important to you to easily meet people, in which case some kind of mixed accommodation might appeal.

Sometimes (not always, obviously) having the option of halls of residence is quite an autism-friendly one. Being in your own, self-contained area while having people around you could be a safe way of engaging with others but maintaining your own space. Or, it might be that the idea of sharing a space such as a cooking or bathroom area is too much to bear.

These are all things that it is well worth taking into consideration when identifying the accommodation option that best suits you. Similar to the points system for choosing an educational institution, you could develop one for assisting in choosing the type of accommodation that best suits your needs. Additional points to take into account include costs (take into account whether bills are included in the fees), location (is it within walking distance of your place of learning, for example), duration of commitment, longer-term availability (e.g. sometimes you may have to move out of halls after your first year), and sensory issues such as noise.

Freshers' week/fortnight

Very often for first year students at university the institution will open a week or two early to welcome new students and host a range of activities known as Freshers' week; this will vary from place to place in terms of duration and the activities involved – so it might be very beneficial to ascertain whether or not this is something that you wish to engage in. Make sure that it is clear to you whether an activity is part of an optional 'getting to know others' one, or whether as part of a specific course there is an expectation to attend – in which case it may be labelled 'orientation' or something similar.

You can usually pick and choose what activities, if any, you wish to engage in – there is no need to engage in all of them by any means. This is where an idea of what causes you anxiety compared to what you might get out of engaging with these activities is useful to consider. The main thing is to remember that Freshers' time is very limited compared to the duration of your course, and while it might help you meet people, it doesn't mean that abstaining from Freshers' activities will mean you won't have the chance to establish friendships/relationships after your course has started.

Lecture theatres

So many things about educational life beyond what you are used to might differ – so you may need to prepare yourself for these changes. For example, you might be used to operating in a relatively small class environment and all of a sudden you are exposed to large groups within a lecture theatre. This is something that you may want to 'practise' prior to your educational experience. Public lectures at universities are not uncommon, so if you know that you are likely to be taught in a lecture theatre, you could get that experience in before you start life as a student.

Group work

Many of you may have a love/hate relationship with working as part of a group, and many courses seem to encourage group activity for a variety of reasons. It might be that you abhor group work, and need to take this into account when choosing your course. If you are on a course on which group activity is mandatory, then it is very useful to be as structured as possible within the group when it comes to allocating work. Many of you would end up taking on way more than you are required to unless it is very clear as to whose responsibility it is to do what. My view is that courses should always have an opt-out clause for group work unless there is an actual need for it as part of the award (see the tips section at the end of this chapter).

Independence

Most of you will need to be more independent on your educational journey than you are used to – but it is well worth working out what is important to you in terms of independent living. There is quite a pressure on young people to 'be independent' – but I am never quite sure just how independent the vast majority of adults actually are. I think it is more important to figure out strengths and weaknesses, so that if there are areas that you are more dependent on, they can be identified along with how you might be supported. This is no different to an adult getting a plumber in to fix a tap – this is a clear example of lack of independence that no one would consider problematic.

If you are the sort of person who struggles in areas that other folk find easy, you should not be made to feel bad about it, nor should you be forced into making yourself be independent in an area that is unnatural or even impossible for you. Don't fall into the trap of societal pressure – being true to your strengths and weaknesses is likely to be much less stressful.

Many educational institutions have support systems to enable students who might find certain areas of independence difficult to access the right support. It is very likely that your strengths in many areas will supersede those of other students, and vice versa – so there is no shame in seeking support for the parts of life that you feel less confident in, while utilizing your strengths elsewhere.

Societies

There will be any number of clubs and societies for you to join, and they may be an exemplary way of meeting people who have similar interests to you. You may find that in life there is an almost unspoken pressure to have a wide range of social contacts – also known as friends. Do not fall into the trap of having to emulate others – you may well be the sort of person who would much prefer to have a small number of close friends, rather than a large number of people who are more akin to acquaintances. More on this later – but for the sake of this section, it could be useful to really make use of the social opportunities that societies offer. If your particular area of interest is not represented by the institution, consider whether it might be beneficial to you to develop it yourself.

One thing that must be noted here – there are growing numbers of educational facilities that either host groups specifically for autistic students (or neurodivergent students) or have students running such groups themselves. I know many students who have found these groups very supportive and beneficial. I am not suggesting that they will be of the same benefit to all of you, and some of you may prefer to avoid them altogether – but for some, they could be a really positive experience and source of support.

Exams/assessments/study

You may be used to an educational system that has a certain period of teaching, followed by either coursework, exams, or a combination of them. It might be the case that this pattern is not dissimilar to your ongoing educational journey, but there are likely to be key differences. These include:

- **Less formal teaching**. In a sense, the higher the level of academic study, the less direct contact you might have with teaching staff. This isn't always the case, of course, but it may well be that you are exposed to fewer teaching hours than you have been used to – and yet you are expected to study at a higher academic level than you have been used to. This requires a certain level of discipline and organization that you may not have encountered before.
- **Onus on independent study**. Similarly, you may be expected to be far more independent and less reliant on direction compared to previous experiences. It might be that this is one of your strengths – but it might also be something that you need to work at in order to achieve what you are capable of. Certainly it is something that you need to be aware of so you know what to expect.
- **Length of submissions**. You may be required to produce work that is longer than you have ever done before. Taking the above two points into consideration, this is where time management and self-discipline are crucially important. It can be incredibly stressful to feel that you are behind, and yet difficult to get started on work that doesn't need to be handed in for several weeks or even months. A study diary might be a useful option; study buddies are also sometimes helpful.

Obviously these are just three of the potential differences – you may be exposed to other ways of teaching and learning. Always take the time to find out as much as you can in terms of what to expect on a course so that your choice is one that suits your needs as much as possible.

Doctoral study

While it is not for everyone, I have a belief that doctoral study can be incredibly autism friendly under the right circumstances. After all, it tends to require extreme levels of attention in an area that is of particular interest to you, to a high degree of detail – all of which might fit very well into your way of engaging. Somewhat frustratingly, our education system tends to be rather linear – get one set of qualifications that are a springboard to the next, which leads to the next, which eventually leads to a doctorate. But if those early qualifications are not suited to your learning style then you may be being 'failed' at an early stage. I am incredibly fortunate to be able to supervise doctoral students; many of those (autistic) doctoral students that I am fortunate enough to know have not followed a traditional educational/academic route.

You are entitled to reasonable adjustments as a doctoral student in the same way as you are within any other educational study – just because you are studying at a doctoral level doesn't diminish your learning needs. Ensuring that you have had an appropriate assessment of need might make a huge difference on your doctoral journey – this should take all your needs into account from day one of your study all the way through to graduation – and very much not forgetting your Viva.

Tips for HE to reduce autistic anxiety

As noted towards the beginning of the chapter, these are suggestions that in my view will be incredibly useful for many of you. They are not a set of requirements for all educational institutions, although in some cases they could be considered a duty to avoid discrimination. I am sure that the list could be expanded exponentially – it's more of a starting point for consideration and, hopefully, progress.

Flexibility of application

Wouldn't it be amazing if there was greater flexibility in how one might apply to an institution? The option of a verbal narrative, for example, rather than a written one – after all, it could be that it's even easier to process listening to an application than reading one!

Alternatives to traditional Freshers' activities

This is really to ensure that there are activities that are more suited to an autistic population on the whole than many of the traditional ways that students are encouraged to engage, early on in their introduction to student life. Making sure that there is an adequate range of activities, not all of which are centred on unpredictability and social interaction, could benefit some of you. I am not suggesting that you may not want to access many of the traditional activities – but unless there is a full range of options it might be that some students are left out.

Range of assessments

This is a big one! As I have written elsewhere, my view is that there is a direct correlation between the amount of flexible options there are available in any given situation, and the likelihood that there is subsequent equality of access. Let's create our eighth suggested reasonable adjustment:

> *There is an understanding that in principle, the more options there are available to the autistic individual to meet any given requirement, the less chance there is of discrimination.*

In relation to assessment, therefore, the wider the range of options, the less risk there is of discrimination. Take the most standard ways of assessing work – which are probably written coursework and written exams. Already it is relatively easy to suggest that if you are the sort of person whose cognitive style is such that written work puts you at a disadvantage, then this limited way of assessment could be a disaster for you. Assessing knowledge should be exactly that – an assessment of knowledge, not specifically an assessment of how effective a person is at writing that knowledge down – there is a very clear distinction between the two. In many cases, giving students alternative options can mean no additional work for staff, but mean the difference between success and failure for the student.

Just by way of example, I am lucky enough to run a Post Graduate Award in Autism – students can submit a written piece of work, or they can do a live presentation, submit a video presentation, or an audio recording. They can even have an interview style interaction with pre-set questions. The options are available to all students so it's a fair system, and for those students who are far more verbally-orientated rather than written, they can choose an option that showcases their knowledge more effectively than the standard written assignment. I am happy to go on record to note that I live in the hope that, one day, I will get to supervise a student who submits a paperless doctorate.

Other assessments, such as presentations live to a group, might cause so much anxiety that it puts you at a distinct disadvantage – again, there could be alternative options such as an independent recording that a student might make that is still a presentation but in an alternative format to a live one within a group setting. This brings me onto the next suggestion:

Institutions have opt-out clauses

Not all educational options are specific to the award that a student might be working towards. Sessions on employability, for example, could be extremely useful to many students – including autistic students. However, unless those sessions are a mandatory part of the academic award, you should be given the opportunity to avoid them if they cause too much stress. Other examples might be team-building exercises, or interview skills. If your sole reason for study is to gain an award, and these other sessions are so stressful that you would choose to leave the course rather than having to endure them, it would make sense to be clear that you should not be forced into engaging with them.

Choice of group work

This has been covered in part – and many institutions encourage group work (among other activities that are meant to broaden your skill set as an adult, see above); however, yet again, unless it is a requisite that you work as part of a group, there needs to be an alternative if group work causes any student anxiety to the point of discrimination. Many of you will enjoy being part of a group – but equally, many of you will be aiming towards a career that you can mostly embark upon as a sole activity. If this is the case, then the 'skills' required for group work might be unnecessary and irrelevant.

I know from experience that these kinds of suggestions can be difficult for the PNT to digest – there is a perceived need for all sorts of skills to be learned; however, it really is quite simple. If the choice is between having a so-called skill forced upon you as part of an academic award, which is not an integral part of that award, and subsequently dropping out due to anxiety, or not learning that skill which may not be relevant to you anyway, and achieving the award – then to my mind the way forward is obvious. And make no mistake – many people will choose to discontinue their studies because they feel they are being forced into situations that are too anxiety-inducing – when those situations are not a necessary part of the course.

Remote options

In a similar vein as the suggestion that there be multiple options for assessments, I feel that the more flexible the options for actual study, the better chance there is of meeting your needs as an autistic student. Having the option of studying remotely has been available for many years, but it is not common to most institutions. During the COVID-19 pandemic, all of a sudden remote learning became the norm, and I am very well aware of the positive impact this has on many autistic students. I am not for one moment suggesting that all of you will prefer to have remote learning options – but I am equally as convinced that some of you will be able to work extremely effectively in a remote or virtual learning space, when you might not be able to access physical face-to-face teaching. In this day and age I feel that all academic institutions should be at least striving towards flexible options around attendance.

Recorded material

Quite simply, if all teaching material is recorded and subsequently made available for the duration of the course, you are likely to be less disadvantaged. You might need to listen to a lecture a number of times to process it, or you may need to listen to it in an environment that is not as distracting as the lecture theatre – whatever the reason, having materials recorded as standard could go a long way towards making sure all students are treated fairly.

Material to be available prior to lectures and afterwards

As above, in my mind this should simply be standard practice. It might not always be possible – but in the main, I expect it should be perfectly reasonable for teaching staff to be organized enough to have material such as presentations available well before the day they actually deliver it. If you are the sort of individual who struggles to look at visual material at the same time as processing auditory information, then having the opportunity to digest lecture slides before the actual lecture could mean you are no longer at a disadvantage.

Option to opt out of direct interaction

Never underestimate the terror of being in the spotlight and having a teacher ask a question directly to you in front of a group. Many of you will have no issue with this – but if you live in constant fear of this happening to the point that it impacts on your ability to learn, then you should have the discreet option of it never happening.

Option of seating

You might be someone who needs to sit at the front of a lecture theatre – which means you don't have to look at anything other than the teacher; or you may need to be right at the back, so you don't feel the weight of everyone's eyes on you; or you may need to be next to the door so that you have a safe exit if required; or you may need to be at the end of the aisle for a similar reason; or you may need a space either side of you for sensory reasons – the list could go on. Whatever your preference, you should be given the opportunity to have your needs met in terms of where you sit.

Email/communication protocol so you know when to expect a reply

Some of you will be the sort of person for whom sending an email when that email requires a response is extremely anxiety-inducing, especially if you do not know when that response might be forthcoming. I realize that it is almost impossible to make any guarantees as regards response times – from emails, voice messages, whatever type of communication is being utilized; however, even a guide around what a student can expect might alleviate some levels of anxiety, so it's worth working towards a clear system with transparent communication.

Option of draft work to be returned on the same day

I imagine that some teaching staff reading this might blanch at the suggestion – but it's not necessarily as onerous as one might think. Some students, on the submission of work that they expect comments on (e.g. draft assignments) can literally go into a state of what I call 'anxiety stasis' – a state of heightened anxiety until such a time as the work is returned. If this is the case, then arranging a mutually convenient time for the work to be submitted and subsequently the work being commented on and returned on the same day could be an absolute game changer for that student. This sounds improbable – but I have known students (of mine) who have suggested that without this option it is likely that they would not have considered the course. I can also tell you that in my experience, most autistic students don't need this option – but for those who do need it, it is almost essential.

Summer visits

As noted in the first half of this chapter, educational opportunities might be scary simply because of the number of unknown factors. I adore the idea of having summer visits to institutions so that prospective students can access teaching environments, libraries, halls of residence and so on to get a feel for what their future student life might be like. The closer this can emulate their future experiences the better – but I suspect that any opportunity to be able to access the institution would be beneficial.

Graduation

Graduation is often a real highlight for successful students. You, on the other hand, might dread the need to access such a day due to sensory overload, to mention just one issue that could be problematic for a graduation ceremony. But you deserve graduation just as much as anyone else – so if there could be virtual access to graduation to ensure that all students are included, so much the better to end your academic career.

7

Employment

Employment is rife with potential issues for you, but I remain convinced that if employment systems themselves were to make adaptations then your life would be considerably improved. Having to endure anxiety as a result of work is not an option that will lead to an enjoyable existence. In fact, much like the anxiety on a day-to-day basis that many of you will have experienced at school, having to suffer from the interminable, grinding, soul-destroying anxiety that might stem from work on a daily basis can have a very adverse impact, both in your daily wellbeing and your longer-term mental health. It is essential, therefore, that your employment situation is as anxiety-free as possible.

I am reasonably convinced that if employers actually realized just how stressful some of you find your working environment, they might do more to help alleviate it. It might even be that you don't realize it yourself – in which case some of the sections earlier on in the book could be useful to gauge whether some of your ongoing anxiety can be traced back to your working environment. In a sense, this chapter is aimed more at your employer than it is at you – after all, if it is the work place that is generating anxiety, surely it is the workplace's responsibility (or, more accurately, whoever has control over the workplace) to do what is reasonable to reduce or eliminate that anxiety. Of course, your employer won't know whether they have a lawful duty to implement reasonable adjustments unless they know that you suffer from work-related autistic anxiety, which means that some level of disclosure is required. You may be in a position of not wanting to disclose, for very good reasons, in which case your employer will be limited in terms of what they can do. Unfortunately, until everyone develops a better understanding of autism, you may still be disadvantaged by preconceptions of autism if you disclose – for example on the application form, or at interview. This goes back to the very first reasonable adjustment suggestion, that there be no assumptions based on the disclosure.

So – from this point on I am writing to your employer/future employer just for the rest of this chapter.

Tips for employers to reduce autistic anxiety

The following are things you might like to consider. I have provided tips in some cases and created stories (all based on real-life examples) in others, each of them making a specific point in relation to employment practice. All of the named individuals are autistic adults.

Applications

Harriet is very keen to secure a job with you. She is eminently capable, hard-working, industrious, and in all probability she would make for an excellent addition to your workforce. Unfortunately, you might never know, as you don't receive an application from her. The reality is, that Harriet's cognitive style is such that filling in application forms, in the format that you have provided online, is next to impossible. She starts off with good intentions but just gets so stressed at trying to work out what needs to go where, why the formatting keeps changing, why some of the boxes that need filling in are the wrong size for the number of words required, why there are not enough lines provided for her home address – practically every aspect of the form is 'wrong' and her mind goes into meltdown trying to cope with it all. Rather than punishing herself in this way she admits defeat, and the application never gets completed.

After your autism training delivered by an autistic trainer, you change the way in which you recruit. Harriet is still diligently searching for work, and realizes that the job she wanted to apply for with you is still vacant. She knows full well that she won't put herself through that traumatic experience again, but clicks on the link anyway, just out of curiosity. She notices immediately (Harriet is very detail orientated and picks up on visual change very quickly – it's one of her many strengths) that the advert looks very different from last time. What stands out is that there are now options for how to apply. Candidates are invited to choose one of the following options:

- Apply online (this is the same option as last time)
- Provide a pre-prepared CV
- Send in an audio recording of yourself identifying your key achievements and strengths
- Create a video of yourself explaining why you feel you are suited to the job
- Create a presentation with voice over about you and your skills profile
- Ask a present or past employer to provide supporting evidence as to why they think you are suited to the job.

Each of the options have clear instructions, including a word and time limit. Harriet is extraordinarily imaginative, which is one of the reasons why the inflexible application form doesn't suit her. She decides to create a presentation that allows her to demonstrate her imaginative artful flair with a pre-recorded voice-over that she has written to go with each of the slides. She thoroughly enjoys the creative process, and this clearly shows in the end product – which you absolutely love, and invite Harriet in to discuss job prospects at the earliest convenience.

Interviews

Idriss has successfully got through to the final stage of applying for a job with you. The competition has been high, but Idriss has stood out at each stage as a candidate who you feel appears way better than any of the other applicants. The final stage is a formal interview with a panel of six people. Each panelist asks three questions each, but only one at a time – in other words a panelist asks a question, then hands over to the next person, until all questions have been asked. Idriss appears confident to start off with and answers the first question competently and with great assurance – you feel that you were right all along, and that he will be just right for the job. However, as each person completes their question and hands on to the next panelist, the less able Idriss appears to be to answer with any level of competence. Finally, he simply sits and declares that he cannot answer any more questions, even though the panelists have not yet asked all of them. It is impossible for you to give Idriss the job based on this apparently inadequate performance.

Idriss sends an email after the interview and explains that as an autistic person he has the ability to process information at exceptional speeds – but the amount of data that he has to process is vastly more than the average person. He also finds it incredibly difficult to switch from listening to one person to listening to another in a short space of time, as he has to completely recalibrate his auditory system to be able to process the 'new' voice accurately; without sufficient time to do this words start getting lost. It's not that he can't process – it's the combination of the sheer volume of data in a room with six other people in it along with the constant switching of voices that cause the difficulty. He articulates in his message that eventually the questions put to him no longer made any coherent sense, at which point he could not answer them.

You discuss this with the panel, all of whom show a great interest in how the autistic brain works, and you invite him back for a second interview. This time the same people are within the same room, but rather than each person asking a question, one spokesperson asks all 18 questions while everyone else sits quietly and listens to Idriss's answers. His initial competence doesn't wane at all, and he answers the last question with just as much coherence and excellence as the first, and is immediately offered the job.

Before moving to the next example, it is well worth asking yourself whether interviews are really a useful way to ascertain suitability for a job. Unless the actual job involves being interviewed or having interview-type discussions, how many of the skills on display during an interview are actually beneficial to the prospective role? Added to this is the complication that interviews are essentially a PNT game with unwritten rules, and one is almost expected to exaggerate some aspects of self and do the opposite for others, rather than being brutally honest (which is more likely for the autistic interviewee) and you might start to wonder whether the interview process itself could be deemed discriminatory.

Job descriptions/person specifications – consider matching skills to work

Jo doesn't apply for jobs when within the job description or person spec she reads that the employee needs to have 'good communication skills'. Jo is eminently competent when communicating via email, but finds the prospect of face-to-face communication or phone conversations utterly soul destroying. As almost all jobs that she feels she could do ask for good communication skills, she is prevented from applying for them.

The reality is that Jo ends up as an exceptional customer service manager. Someone who knows Jo well realizes what the issue is, and persuades a company to tweak the job description to ask for 'good electronic communication skills' – which actually reflected the job far more accurately, as the job is entirely based on providing online customer service; Jo never has to use the phone or engage with a customer face to face.

This example is just a micro-version of a much bigger problem within employment when it comes to many autistic adults. So many job descriptions and person specifications are generalized and vague, asking all candidates to be good in a whole range of areas, many of which might not be particularly applicable. Understanding that the skills profile of your autistic employee is likely to be spiky, and changing what their role is to play to their strengths not only decreases their anxiety and makes for a more productive employee, but it just makes good common sense. We all know perfectly well that the bits of the job that we are best at tend to be the easiest and the quickest to achieve – so why are we wasting time trying to force people to engage in work that others are way more competent at, when an employee could be so much more effective working on their own particular area that they excel at?

Is there any need for structured time frames in the working day?

Consider whether there needs to be a strict start, finish, break time, and/or lunch time for your employees. Obviously this will be extremely dependent on the kind of organisation that you are involved in – however, I suspect as a hangover of long-term traditions, many jobs have designated start and finish times, including set times for breaks, that are of no practical relevance. But some autistic employees might have a much more effective system of working outside of these set times. Many jobs are, in fact, not time orientated – in which case perhaps you could consider working with your employee around what you expect them to do on any given day, and give them the flexibility as to how they go about doing it.

Of course, you need to take employment law into account regarding work time, but there can still be a level of flexibility that might better suit your employee. Many of your employees may prefer to take a break at a different time to other co-workers, for example, or prefer to have a shorter break at lunch and finish a bit earlier as a result. Some might like to come to work a couple of hours before anyone else to enjoy the peace that that offers, or stay after everyone else has left. The point is, if the job is around completing tasks rather than completing a timed 'shift' then there could be all sorts of autism-friendly flexible working opportunities that could considerably reduce anxiety – as well as quite probably increasing the productivity of your employee.

How to set expectations

Karl is so frequently late in his production of reports that it is becoming a problem. He almost always misses the deadline, and the reports themselves are so detailed (accurate but with too much detail) that they are not very efficient or effective. When you have a meeting with Karl about this he becomes extremely upset. It turns out that when he was being prepared for the job he was told by his line manager at the time to 'do as detailed a job as you possibly can in report writing'. Karl is very honest and likes to do as he has been asked, and so has made every effort to be as detailed as he can in writing reports, which often means that they take much longer than he is allocated time for. When questioned further, it becomes apparent that Karl frequently takes reports home with him and works on them in the evenings, just to make sure that he fulfills the expectation that they are as detailed as possible. Karl has got to a point where he is in a constant state of stress worrying about the reports, their level of detail, and the fact that he has to either compromise on what he has been asked to do, or to miss deadlines – both options causing considerable anxiety.

In order to support Karl you explain to him that the expectations have now changed, and you give him a template for report writing that he can use as a basis for the level of detail required. Karl now provides highly effective reports, usually well before the time at which they are due, and is no longer taking work home with him.

How to line manage

I genuinely believe that if you line manage an autistic employee, then it should be regarded as absolutely reasonable that you have a good understanding of their needs in order to best reduce risk of discrimination. And yet how many line managers do not really seem to understand the needs of their autistic employees? So many times I have been told horrific stories whereby a line manager essentially ignores the fact that their employee is autistic, and expects her to do everything in the same way as everyone else, even though she continually reminds her line manager of her needs.

I shudder at times when there are 'autism awareness' events at work, or within society. Autistic adults need understanding and acceptance, not awareness. Awareness 'training' might even cause the autistic employee even more problems – after all, how much can anyone really learn about one autistic individual's needs by going on an 'awareness' course?

Line management needs to be so specific to each autistic employee that it is impossible to articulate exactly what a good line manager might look like. What might be fantastic practice for one person could spell disaster for another. In fact, this is suggested reasonable adjustment nine:

> Never assume that the needs of any two autistic adults are automatically the same.

What this means is that you should never think that just because something worked really well for an autistic person in your employment last year, it will work just as well for a different autistic person in your employment this year. So, line managers need to have a level of understanding and acceptance of their employee's autistic needs, not just awareness of them.

For some, promotion should not include additional line management responsibilities

Luca is having an absolute disaster at work. Before his promotion he was clearly by far the best employee in the company at that level, and he was automatically promoted as a direct result. However, ever since his promotion his ability to do his job has declined rapidly, and he expresses his desire to hand his notice in.

Instead of accepting Luca's notice, you decide to do some investigation as to what the problem is, and you diligently begin to work out how Luca has ended up in such a difficult position. You learn that while Luca is excellent at a particular job, the assumption that this should mean he should then manage other people to do that job effectively is not an assumption that holds any validity. In fact, you feel awful when you realize that in reality, after promotion, the actual job that Luca has to do is vastly different to the one he excels at. Rather than being able to get on with a job that Luca is extremely good at independently, all of a sudden Luca has to engage with others, and give them direction – these are not things that Luca is at all comfortable with, and he has got to a point whereby he cannot bear the stress any longer, so is seeking to leave his role. Rather than losing such a valuable member of staff, you are able to agree with Luca that he still gets his promotion as a result of his valuable contribution, but he is allocated work that doesn't involve direct line management, and that is more in line with his actual skill set. The result is that Luca remains a happy employee, and the company retains one of their best members of staff.

Social activities – Christmas parties, etc.

It should be absolute standard practice, in my view, to have to proactively opt *in* to extra curricula social activities that are not a part of one's job. Currently, it is frequently the case that one has to actively opt *out* – which places the onus of responsibility, not to say the spotlight, onto those who wish nothing less than to be left alone in peace and quiet to get on with their jobs in the proper manner, while avoiding the horrific prospect of having to socially engage with people who are only acquaintances purely by circumstance and chance.

Don't assume an employee wants to progress

Martha spends hours agonizing over her annual review. Every year it causes her incredible anxiety, and every year the result of the review is that she has to complete yet another course that adds to her CV. No one at work realizes the stress that this causes Martha. One day her line manager changes, and instead of having to fill in what is known as the 'pre-review template', Martha's line manager asks Martha how she would best be suited having a review. Martha is astounded – she has never been asked this before. She explains to her new line manager that in previous years when filling in the form, the biggest issue was having to respond to the question that directly requested what additional skills Martha wanted to gain, along with a list of courses that were available in various different areas. Martha's reality is that while she loves her job, she has zero desire to 'climb the ladder' or develop new skills that she feels are unnecessary and distracting. So, each year, she is forced to choose an option of attending a course which is hard enough, but she then has to waste her time actually attending the course.

Martha's line manager, much to Martha's satisfaction, agrees that Martha no longer has to attend courses, and doesn't have to develop herself in any way other than how she chooses to herself.

Please note – this is just one example; many autistic employees might very much want to progress in their careers; however, it is wrong simply to assume that all people want to progress, or should progress if it is not their wish.

Consider a neurodiversity group

There can be safety in numbers – or, at the very least, a great source of comfort being with others who might share similar views and ways of engaging with the world as you. Having a neurodiversity group can make an enormous difference to an autistic employee. Meeting in confidence in a safe space and the group being supported by the employer may take minimal effort and resource, and yet the positive impact might be considerable.

Where a person physically needs to be

There is growing flexibility in working environments around aspects such as working from home. Many autistic employees will be vastly more effective and less stressed in their jobs if the physical environment is taken into account. Chapter 3 identifies many of the issues here – suffice to say, if there are flexible options for your autistic employees that allow them to be less anxious as a result, make those options available.

8

Tips for you and society

There is so much that still needs to be done and, in line with the themes elsewhere in this book, my belief is that most of those adaptations need to be undertaken by others in society, rather than you. Of course there is always a level of compromise, but I feel that too often all of the onus of responsibility to adapt and change to 'fit in' lies on your shoulders, which might simply exacerbate an anxious situation. If others are able to make adaptations without associated anxiety, as opposed to 'simply' insisting on you having to change yourself (which actually increases anxiety), then the way forward seems obvious to me.

This chapter is written to a general reading audience, rather than specifically directed at you (the autistic reader). This is because much of the narrative identifies various issues that might cause anxiety, with some suggestions for change – and many of those changes will not (or should not) be your responsibility.

Communication

To be absolutely clear from the outset – communication is a two-way process. Far too often the autistic adult appears to be the one to 'blame' in that they are labelled as being impaired in communication, or too literal, or too blunt (the list is a long one!). But understanding communication through the autism lens suggests that in many cases it is more a case of what could be referred to as a 'communication clash' – whereby one person's style of communication clashes with a different communicative style, leading to misunderstanding or lack of understanding altogether. This goes both ways, I suspect – in other words, many autistic styles of communication will lead to a lower level of comprehension for the PNT – and vice versa. As it currently stands, many autistic adults are the ones for whom the pressure is on to learn PNT communication and change their own natural way of communicating and understanding in order to better 'fit'. But it might not take too much for the wider population to make some simple changes, based on a better autism understanding, that ultimately benefits everyone.

Phones

It is always a good idea to establish clear boundaries. Does the autistic adult use a phone comfortably? By this I mean answers to the following questions might be beneficial:

1 Does speaking on a phone cause anxiety in a general sense?
2 Do unexpected phone calls cause anxiety?
3 Does the individual prefer to know what the time frame of an expected phone call might be?

Answers to these simple questions can do much to alleviate anxiety. Imagine if you live in fear of your phone ringing – not because you have a problem with using the phone, but because of the fear of the unexpected/unknown. Even a call from a known contact at an unexpected time can trigger anxiety – a withheld number might be even worse. This is not to suggest that all autistic adults fall into this category, but some will. Now imagine if everyone who has that person's number agrees that they will only ever ring at a prearranged time, or will send a 'warning' text in advance. All of a sudden the chances of anxiety being triggered reduces hugely. Some autistic adults simply turn their phone off – but I also know people who have tried this as a tactic and it just increases anxiety, as there is subsequent constant rumination over who might be trying to call, and what voicemail messages might be being left for when the phone is turned back on.

Texts

Just a brief note here – some autistic adults may not always know when to start and/or end a text 'conversation' – after all, there doesn't appear to be many (or any) rules that everyone can agree on. This could cause anxiety, so if you know someone who might worry about such things, it's well worth establishing some rules of your own to determine what is acceptable to both of you.

Email

Email exchanges are so commonplace these days that many people simply take them for granted without any particular thought whatsoever. Not so for some autistic adults who might stress quite considerably around what to include, what not to include, what 'tone' to use; not only that, but I know plenty of individuals who fret massively once an email has been sent, worrying over whether it was 'ok' or not. Sometimes those individuals might follow up with another email asking for reassurance that the previous email was 'ok' – didn't cause any offence and so on, but even this system can cause additional stress as the person then has yet another email to worry about. This is the sort of thing that, if you don't have the same sorts of worries, then it might be very difficult to understand. But there will be people for whom this scenario is all too real, and the impact it can have is massive – and massively negative.

I can't speak for all of you, but my way of working is simply to let people know that if they have any concerns or worries, then I am perfectly happy to provide reassurance if that is what is required, and I won't think any less of a person for asking. This can be enough to alleviate anxiety.

Types of communication – social v factual

There are plenty of different types of communication, but there is a difference between social communication and factual infor-mation exchanges (with some overlap at times). Many autistic adults will be fabulous at factual exchanges, especially if questions posed are clear, unambiguous, and not dependent on additional information. Actually, while I am on this subject, please – if you are asking an autistic adult a question which is in a questionnaire format or similar, in other words no one else is present to provide any other information, please do as much as you can to avoid the response being, 'well – it depends!' – as this is mightily frustrating to many people.

Anyway – a relatively simple rule might be that within a work context you try to focus on work-related issues, and outside work you focus on social issues. It very much helps if you make the effort to identify what a person feels comfortable talking about – and what they are not comfortable talking about. It may be that you have very little idea as to how much impact asking an innocuous question might have, as so many autistic adults are tremendously adept at hiding how anxious they are – but it is definitely worth trying to establish from an early stage what the social boundaries could be for communication.

Truthfulness and being believed

It is a myth that autistic people cannot lie! However, many autistic people do find it very difficult to say things that they feel are not true, however harsh that reality might seem. It might also be that they tend to accept whatever it is that you say – in which case you should take responsibility for making sure that what you say is as accurate and unambiguous as possible. Many autistic adults love language, some to the point of feeling extremely anxious when they feel that language is being abused in some way. This might sound like hyperbole – but it isn't!

In a similar vein, many autistic adults, when they tell their version of the truth, may be incredibly stressed if they are not believed. Some will have learned the hard way to suppress their truth as a result of these experiences as a child – which comes with its own anxiety. Having trusted people who accept that (at the very least) the autistic person is absolutely telling their truth can be wonderfully liberating; having people dismiss out of hand what is being said can be incredibly damaging.

Lies and the need to understand that there are different scales

One thing that can be massively useful to learn is that lies are not always the same – in other words there is a sliding scale of lies that might range from a 'white lie' which is actually meant to be kind, all the way through to extreme dishonest manipulation. If, as an autistic adult, you respond the same way irrespective of intent, because 'a lie is a lie' then you may be suffering huge levels of distress that may not be necessary.

Tips for others to reduce anxiety related to communication

- **Ask for preferred communication.** It is always worth considering that someone might have preferred forms of communication, and that these may differ depending on the circumstances. Having that conversation may be really useful, for both parties, to identify communicative preferences.
- **Be accurate.** While I have identified above that many people will struggle with lies (or perceived lies), learning that what has been said may not be malicious, even though it may not be true, and making sure that what you say is as linguistically accurate as possible, might go some way towards a reduction in miscommunication and, therefore, anxiety. If you listen to a PNT conversation, you might be somewhat surprised at how linguistically inaccurate or ambiguous the narrative is; imagine, then, if you were extremely accurate yourself and therefore processed that narrative in a very different way, how confusing that could be.
- **Understand the need for shared meaning of words and concepts.** Many people will make assumptions that what they understand by a particular word or concept is the same for others within a communicative exchange. However, this is not always the case. It is definitely worth having those discussions so that you are aware of possible misunderstandings. Just a quick example – imagine the distress you might inadvertently cause if, during an induction for new employees at work, you state that 'all of us here strive for perfection every day at work, and we accept nothing less' – this might be meant to be inspiring and forward thinking; however, if your autistic employee hears that they are expected to be *perfect in everything they do* at work – and, if they are not, they will stand out because everyone else is somehow being perfect and therefore accepted, just imagine the strain that the individual will be put under.
- **Accept when you are in the wrong.** If an autistic person challenges you, always take the time to work out whether they do, in fact, have a valid point. It is so frustrating to suggest to

someone that a better way of phrasing it might be [whatever it is] only for the immediate reaction to be something along the lines of, 'Well, you know what I mean' or, 'It doesn't really matter'; if that person is genuinely trying to help and you dismiss them 'out of hand' it can be hurtful, and difficult to understand.

- **Allow time for processing if needed**. It might be that some individuals may need time to process communication as they are processing so much in addition to what you are saying. If this is the case then acknowledge that (internally – not literally) and respect that the individual is not being difficult, it is a necessity. Consider the sensory environment at all times, as this will almost definitely impact on processing speeds for communication.

- **Recognize that communication will differ at different times.** Just because a person has superb processing and abilities to communicate in some circumstances, do not make the assumption that this will always be the case. It is the same for you – if you are in a highly pressured situation and you are extremely anxious then it is likely that your communicative ability might diminish. For the autistic person who may be anxious anyway, with all the additional sensory issues to deal with, communication might be a challenge way more than you might ever have realized.

Relationships

I think another book is required – I am certain that a whole book on relationships could easily be written, and I certainly don't have the space within this one to do it justice. However, this section is aimed at any partners of autistic adults, with just a few suggestions as to how you might alleviate anxiety.

Accept autistic identification 100 per cent

It may sound like odd advice, but so many people seem to almost forget that their partner is autistic. Remind yourself that they are! However good they are at hiding their identity, however much they might appear to cruising along without any issue, the reality is that being autistic is a lived experience, it can't be switched on and off, so you being constantly aware and supportive can be life-changing. Learn alongside your partner what impact autism has on life – discovery can be a wonderful thing, and discovery together can be immeasurably appealing. Of course it might be that you are both autistic – the same rules apply! Remembering that you are likely to share all sorts of experiences, but that you will also differ in some ways, is essential.

Believe what they say in relation to experience

Don't dismiss your partner's experiences just because you don't share them yourself! If your partner is brave enough to share their anxiety with you, don't think it's not as bad as they make out, or think that it can't possibly be that anxiety-inducing just because you find the same thing easy. I really like the parallels here with genuine phobias; if someone is terrified, for example, of spiders, many people will accept this at a conceptual level, especially if they are not keen on spiders themselves. However, it might not be until you witness the devastating impact of a spider on that person in a real-life scenario that you actually grasp just how distressing it is – at which point you take them even more seriously. However, if someone confides in you that what they find distressing is the sound of the post being delivered, it might be that your own experience is such a far cry from theirs that it is difficult to take them seriously. This doesn't detract from the fact that many autistic adults will be triggered by events that might seem trivial to others – that remind them of something in the past that holds its own trauma. It might be a word, an experience, or a sensory process such as smell – these things need to be taken just as seriously as the aforementioned spider.

Proactively discuss anxiety, causes and possible solutions

Empathy is a lovely thing to demonstrate to your autistic partner, but it might be difficult, especially if you are not autistic yourself. But demonstrating that you are aware of the potential issues that your partner might face and proactively being supportive can be incredibly helpful to an autistic adult. Knowing that you are there for them, even if you don't necessarily fully understand what it means to have autistic anxiety, is a precious thing indeed.

Recognize that you may have to compromise on certain things

There must be pros and cons to almost every partnership – and this can also be said of a partnership with your autistic individual. But it might be that the sorts of compromises you make are somewhat different to those within a PNT relationship. For example, it might be that your partner needs downtime after a social occasion – and that the downtime must be taken alone. Sometimes it is too easy to take this personally, as opposed to understanding that it is a requisite for your autistic partner, not an indication that they don't want to spend time with you. There could be so many other examples – this is just one to make the point.

Fight their corner if necessary

Having someone who is able to advocate for you when necessary can be truly magnificent. Knowing both of your strengths and weaknesses so that you can complement each other can work incredibly effectively. Knowing that you might need to explain things to others because it is too stressful for your partner, taking that pressure off them, can go a long way to reducing anxiety. Stepping in when you realize that your partner's stress is rising can also be an absolute boon.

Be their trusted anchor

Being able to trust someone explicitly is probably difficult for many people, but if your partner has had a lifetime of being let down (as many autistic people have been) then having you to trust in could literally be the best thing in their life. Having someone there who accepts you (the autistic partner) and doesn't judge you for who you are, who is willing to fight on your behalf, who understands that your ways of doing things is just different, not bad – these are things that can change an adulthood of lonely anxiety to a sense of strength and acceptance. It might be that, with that level of trust, your partner is able to face all the injustices of the rest of the world in the absolute knowledge that they can rely completely on you.

Passionate interests and routines

So – many autistic adults will have routines and/or passionate interests. Sometimes these might appear to overlap; sometimes the individual will be more orientated towards a passionate interest than a routine. Sometimes passionate interests are referred to as obsessions - which seems to me to convey a negative implication, which is why I prefer the term 'passionate interests'. Passionate interests must not be confused with Obsessive Compulsive Disorder (OCD) which is something else altogether. However, on the face of it, engaging with a passionate interest could be misinterpreted as OCD, so this is something to be wary of. Confusing matters even more is that OCD does appear to be more common in the autistic population than the PNT. Irrespective of the commonalities with OCD, though, passionate interests are usually extremely positive. They can be incredibly motivating and hugely rewarding. They can offer eons of absorbing and fruitful time for the autistic person. And can be a 'go to' activity so one never gets bored. The anxiety associated with a passionate interest is often generated by others' attitude towards it, especially if the immediate assumption is that it is somehow unhealthy to have such a degree of focus on one particular interest. Anxiety might be generated as a result of:

- Others assuming that the topic is inappropriate
- Others assuming that too much time is taken on it
- Others making a person feel bad about enjoying it so much.

Others assuming that the topic is inappropriate

For whatever reason, others might assume a topic is not appropriate for a person. This might be because they feel it is age-inappropriate or maybe the subject matter itself makes them feel uncomfortable. Of course, some interests could definitely be deemed 'wrong', for example if they are unlawful! However, at a totally objective level, however much others find it difficult to get interested in the topic themselves, it should be understood that many passionate interests, while possibly needing some boundaries under some circumstances, are actually perfectly harmless. In fact, very often the positives of having a passionate interest outweigh the negatives by a huge margin, especially if the negatives are more around other people not really understanding the joy of the activity.

Others assuming that too much time is taken on it

I absolutely accept that if a person is so engaged that they are making themselves ill in some way, or it has taken over to such a degree that it is negatively impacting on life in some way, then there is a problem. However, just because a person spends a lot of time engaging with an activity should not automatically mean that there is an issue. In other areas of life people are praised for their dedication in certain areas – but when an autistic person displays that very same dedication in an area that is not deemed of interest to others, then very often the suggestion is that they need to limit their time and do something else. The point is, unless that 'something else' is meaningful and useful to the individual, then why would they ever contemplate replacing valuable time dedicated to a passionate interest to another activity that doesn't serve a legitimate purpose to them?

Others making a person feel bad about enjoying it so much

So much stress is caused to autistic adults by others making them feel bad at being so interested and engaged in their passionate interest. To be made to feel bad as a direct result of being so absolutely enamoured and fascinated by something seems borderline cruel – just because others might not share that passion should not diminish the individual's enthusiasm, which should be applauded and supported, not ridiculed.

Routines are often as a result of wanting some level of predictability and stability in life. Having global stability is a wonderful state to be in, but I fear that many of you (I am back to referring to you as the autistic reader) will not exist in such a state.

Global stability relies on you feeling comfortable with day-to-day existence, rather than being in a negatively aroused emotional state (very often anxiety) much of the time.

This whole book is written in a way that might help you identify what those anxieties are and how they might be reduced, not least for society and others in your life to take note of the impact that the environment has and what needs to change to reduce your anxiety and allow you to feel emotionally stable. In the meantime, it is likely that you will rely on other aspects of your life in order to balance out that instability; routines can be an excellent way of creating predictable, controllable times in the day in which you can relax in the full knowledge that you know exactly what is happening, in what order, and with what outcome. Woe betide anyone who tries to interfere with your routine! Others need to understand just how important those routines are for you. Trying to get you to break your routine if it is there for a very specific, positive reason is unlikely to be successful and is not rooted in an in-depth understanding of what that routine means to you!

9
Balance

So – this chapter is all about the balance of daily life, and how you might go about understanding and working towards a healthy balance between the demands of living and your emotional state. These are all just suggestions – there is clearly no obvious answer to reducing your anxiety, otherwise you would have discovered it by now and I wouldn't have written this book! I have no doubt that some of what you will read in this chapter will not be particularly relevant to you – but if just one sentence gives you a way of reducing your anxiety then writing the whole book will have been worth it!

This final chapter will cover possible issues that relate directly to your living experiences that have not been covered thus far, including some of the positives you might find in being yourself.

Understanding others

One aspect of life that can cause no end of stress is the utter bewilderment that is the PNT – for many of you (and I hope the PNT will forgive me here) the PNT make very little sense, and cause no end of anxiety simply for behaving in the way in which they do. The games the PNT play, the ways in which the PNT communicate, the ways in which the PNT conduct themselves – never underestimate just how trying it is to work out just what is going on, much of the time. Why do the PNT lie so frequently (or at least say things that they do not really seem to believe)? Why might they say one thing to one person and then the complete opposite to another? Why do they insist on social chit-chat that seems to contain no useful information whatsoever? Why can't they focus on one detail for hours on end without getting bored? Why does the PNT lack the urge to dive into a cat's tummy for a full fur facial? If, by the way, you are PNT reading this and resent the generalization and 'othering' language in this brief section, please note that I have written it in this way quite deliberately, and I do hope you will forgive me. After all, it is usually the way that autistic people are written about much of the time.

There is a lack of formal education around how to understand the PNT, and yet I feel that it is a very useful skill to have. To be able to intellectualize why a person is behaving in a manner that seems unusual to you, to provide answers to you with PNT theory – might make your life a lot easier to live. I find it fascinating that many of the PNT are very keen to theorize about autism, to intellectually understand autistic behaviour so that they better understand you as an individual – and yet no one seems as worried about giving you the same opportunities in reverse.

Understanding your autistic self

In a similar vein, if you are autistic and you don't have an excellent understanding as to how autism impacts on you, then it will be that much harder to recognize what causes you anxiety and reduce risk of poor decision making. Suggestion for best practice is that when any autistic person is identified as autistic, they are provided with the necessary support to fully understand what that identity means to them.

The way in which you might be supported is likely to differ, depending on your circumstances. I find that some adults really enjoy studying autism as an academic subject, while others prefer to read other people's stories, or discuss autism with like-minded people. Whatever your source of information, the key thing is that it is accurate and trustworthy – so be very careful what you read and listen to. Just a quick note – always remember that while you share an identity with other autistic adults, you will not be exactly the same as them. You are not an imposter!

Why do you mask? Pros and cons of masking; long-term impacts of masking

Masking might seem like an excellent way of getting along in life. Some of you will be so used to a lifetime of masking that it might even be difficult not to. But masking is tiring – and doing it over long periods of time can lead to untenable levels of exhaustion. Yes, it might help in the short term to get through a particular experience, but it will take something out of you. Until the rest of the world catches up with autism understanding and acceptance, you might feel that you do need to keep masking at certain times if the overall outcome benefits you. So long as you are aware of what it takes out of you, so that you can utilize masking only when absolutely necessary, and you make sure that you have plenty of time to recover; pretending to be someone you are not is potentially damaging, so being very aware of its impact is important. The long-term implications of masking might be dire indeed – I know people who have lost their sense of self and identity because they have felt forced into pretending to be someone else for such a long time.

Balance

Balance – this chapter is all about balance, and making sure that you have a good, healthy balance between the necessities of living and the demands thereof, and your own wellbeing. Everyone, autistic or not, will have difficult times in life and problems on a day-to-day basis. If you suffer from ongoing anxiety then it is far more important for you to balance that out with as much energy as possible dedicated to not being in that state of anxiety. This is a fine balancing act in itself, but I would suggest that the notion of balance is an extremely important one, short-term and long-term.

Balance is all about overall pros and cons – is the energy that you put into something worth the outcome? Always having this in mind will help with your decision making – and this way of working out options could be a very useful way forward that many people don't consider. Take the previous section on masking – asking yourself the question 'In the short and long term, is masking of benefit to me in a specific situation?' might not be something that you've considered before. Working out all of the pros and cons that you are aware of and then asking yourself the same question might allow you to think about your situation in a slightly (or even majorly) different light. Such balance can be applied across the board, from whether or not to disclose to what activity to engage in.

How to relax

I struggled to work out whether to include this section as I didn't want to come across either as patronizing nor as advocating a way of being that others might consider problematic – but in light of the above section, on balance I decided that it is a necessary component of this chapter. Some of you will choose to relax in ways that others could consider a problem – even though you don't have a problem with it, it's not harmful to others, and it's not illegal. In these situations, as above, it is all about balance, along with quality of life. In order to try and avoid anything overly controversial, I will proffer myself as an example. I like to relax by triathlon training – swimming, biking and running. I am very well aware that in doing so I spend time away from people who might prefer it if I was with them (unlikely, but a possibility), I am fully aware that I am sometimes more grumpy when I've injured myself, or I am in pain as a result of all the wear and tear on my body, and I am absolutely certain that I have increased anxiety (which very often results in nightmares and, subsequently, disrupted sleep); however, on balance I am absolutely convinced that there are currently no alternatives that are a better option. I am sure that while there are anxieties around training and racing, I would be far worse off if I didn't engage in exercise at all, and the quality of life I have which subsequently includes quality time with others, is way better than if I was to lead a more sedentary lifestyle. Your way of relaxing may well differ from mine – but the principle of balance is still the same.

Being alone is fine

This may go without saying, but many people feel so much pressure to be with others – be they friends or family or a partner. This appears to be accepted as a societal norm – however, some of you will regard alone time as a necessity to balancing out the pressures of social engagement. Wanting to be alone is not the same as some kind of demonstration that you don't want to be with someone. Unfortunately, some people will think that there is a link between you wanting to be alone and you not wanting to be with them. This is absolutely not automatically the case. I feel that many of the PNT make this assumption but need to understand that, within the autistic population, being alone could simply be a way of allowing anxiety to decrease and actually enables more quality social time with others when the time comes.

Advocacy – allow others to help

Part of the journey of discovery (of autistic identification) is getting to know yourself better, including identifying areas that you might struggle with. Everyone has aspects of life that they could do with support in – and it is a much more efficient way of being to allow others to assist in areas that you find difficult, especially when they might find those tasks easy. It might even be that you set up a barter system whereby you provide the input in areas that you are skilled at, while they do the same in reverse.

Having a genuine advocate, as mentioned previously, can be so incredibly useful. Having a range of people whom you can rely on for various different things might also be an absolute luxury – but many autistic adults seem reluctant to allow others to give them support, in whatever way. Independent living is fine – but there must be some limits, otherwise taking on the world all on your own could prove to be too much.

Blame culture may not be helpful

Sometimes we all have to accept that things are the way that they are – this is not in the slightest bit defeatist, it is more realistic than anything else. I am very much an enthusiastic seeker of change for the better – but also recognize that as things currently stand, they are not ideal for you. It might be that you feel that someone (or some people/institution/organization) needs to shoulder blame for issues that you face; this may well be the case in many situations, but sometimes circumstances are such that difficulties arise through no one's fault – either blaming yourself for this or blaming others is lost energy. It is far more effective to work out what battles to fight and when to fight them – again, it is all about balance.

Knowing your strengths and weaknesses

In a similar vein as the section on advocacy, it is well worth keeping a close eye on your strengths and weaknesses – but, in addition to this, realizing that they are likely to be fluid. Learning how to listen to your self and the signals that you give off can massively change the effective spread of energy to reach maximum potential. So, if you are a morning person, it might be that those early hours are when you are at the most productive in a particular way – but trying to complete the exact same task in the evening might take twice as long, and drain twice as much energy. This can be such a massive realization for many people – and you should allow yourself the opportunity not to engage in activity if it is counter-productive.

Meaningful activity

This is so individual – and yet so important. You might have one or more activities that you feel that you can rely on to de-stress – others have written about various things that might be included here, the seemingly 'go to' currently being 'mindfulness' – but my belief is that it is so specific to you as an individual that it could be misleading to make suggestions. Whatever your meaningful activity is, make it precious. However much others might suggest that you could be spending more productive time doing something else, make sure that you allocate time to your meaningful activity at a frequency and duration that provides the right level of balance – in other words, it fulfills its purpose of relaxing you, but doesn't take up so much time that you become under-productive elsewhere. When people suggest that your activity is without purpose, remember that what they actually mean is that *they* don't find it purposeful – which you can safely ignore as irrelevant.

Allocation of time to others/activities

Ok – so this may seem counter-intuitive or contradictory to the last section, but actually I hope it ties in neatly. It may well be useful to identify the minimum amount of time that you are required – in whatever context, for example spending time with a partner. This need not be 'set in stone' – but if you know that something simply has to be done on a day-to-day basis, such as walking your goose (my own real-life example, by the way), then that time has to be set aside. Time within a day is finite – there is only so much to go around. Being confident and competent at allocating that time, however odd it might seem to others, can be a way of keeping anxiety to a minimum. Of course, this doesn't mean that you only ever have to spend that amount of time with your partner!

Spoons/matches/burnout

In a sense this covers some of the more specific aspects that I have already identified, but it is such a useful concept that I have allocated it its own section. I am not the 'owner' of spoon theory or the concept of 'burning matches' but they are such brilliant ways of understanding energy I will borrow them for a short while.

In spoon theory, the idea is that you wake up or start a specific period of time with a finite number of spoons – which will depend on how you are feeling at the time. As time moves on each spoon – an allocation of a unit of energy – must be used for specific activities. This is fine so long as you have plenty of spoons – but if you start the day with only a few spoons (for example if you are still suffering from a social hangover having had to engage with a dinner party the evening before) then your energy will likely either be depleted early on, or you will have to choose not to use your spoons for various activities for fear of running out. I absolutely love this concept because it is such a fantastic way of understanding that energy is not limitless, and your spoons will be dictated by any number of aspects of life that many others won't even realize. Anxiety, for example, is a devourer of spoons – so living with anxiety almost automatically decreases the number of spoons you might have on a day-to-day basis.

Burning matches is an analogy often used for triathlon racing, and there are some subtle differences to spoon theory. The idea is that at the start of a race you have a certain number of matches, which are akin to how fit you might be in each discipline. There will be an ongoing 'slow burn' of matches throughout the race, as the physical activity is non-stop. However, there will also be bursts of activity that burn your matches at a quicker rate – cycling uphill, or pushing yourself out from transition. If you are a swim-fit person but not so good on the bike, then the bike leg might take more matches than the swim. You have some level of control over the matches, based on how much training you have done, how familiar you are with the course, and whether you want to simply finish the triathlon, or try to beat a personal best. At the end of the race any leftover matches must be thrown away. So, the best racers make all the right decisions and cross the line as their last match burns away – they have been the most efficient. Some triathletes end up wasting matches because they haven't used them, but the athletes who burn all their matches before the finish line, never get to finish. This latter group is to be avoided at all costs.

The magic of both of these analogies is that it can help (so long as others are receptive to the idea) people understand that by not engaging in an activity, you are not being lazy, or disrespectful, or not making the effort – you literally are in the mode of self-preservation. Going back to spoon theory . . . If you were to use up your spoons and then have to start creating spoons out of nothing, this will likely lead to burnout, whereby you experience negative energy levels and cannot do anything but recover. This is so important, perhaps I should have started the book with it – because it may well be the case that you make such a huge effort to do what is expected of you that you go into a negative spoon deficit, *but no one else knows it*. Take attending a day of lectures at university, for example. You know that there is an expectation that you attend four lectures, each between an hour and two hours (totalling six hours), with breaks in between (three of them) including time allocated for lunch. It is an average day for you, which means that you have nine spoons.

Each hour of lecture takes a spoon; each break takes a spoon; eating lunch with others takes a spoon; you are already in spoon deficit, and that is before a single person even speaks to you (and we all know how much social communication gobbles up those spoons). You end the day with a severe spoon deficit, digging deep into yourself to simply get by. *The fact that you subsequently need a three-day recovery period to replenish your spoon allocation goes unnoticed by everyone else.* This leads to the very real, very dangerous notion that you are perfectly fine, and perfectly able to attend a full day of lectures – which is absolutely not the case at all. This is, then, a double whammy – not only are you in a terrible state of spoon deficiency, others have made the very wrong assumption that there are no issues with attending lectures.

So – working out how you might build up your stock of spoons/matches, and understanding what allocation is required, and when, and trying to ensure that there is always an emergency spare spoon or match for when you least expect to need it, could mean you are less at risk of burnout. Just as importantly, getting others to understand that this is the way in which you operate, might make them a whole lot more understanding when you decline that coffee invitation.

Allowing yourself to be autistic

This may seem a bit of a no-brainer – but it is so important to be yourself, to allow yourself to be your authentic autistic self, and find the space, time, and even company in which to do so. The closer you manage to be to your authentic self, the more likely it is that you will be content. Three statements that I for one believe are factually accurate:

- The better *you* know yourself and accept who you are, the more likely it is that you will be content.
- The better that *others* know you and accept who you are, the more likely it is that you will be content.
- The better that *society* as a whole understands and accepts who you are, the more likely it is that you will be content.

Being part of the tribe

This isn't for everyone, but I know plenty of people who, post-identification, have discovered that there are enough like-minded people, either for direct contact or online support, to make their lives immeasurably more beneficial. The concept of belonging, that many of you might feel is not something that is frequently experienced, can be one that you might discover when you fit in with your autistic tribe. The absolute paradise of being utterly accepted and understood as an autistic adult should never be underestimated.

The joys of being autistic

Before I end, I just wanted to acknowledge those hundreds of people whom I have been so lucky to know. Sometimes for several years, sometimes fleetingly. There absolutely can be a joy in being autistic, without a shadow of a doubt. If your shadow is that of constant anxiety, I very much hope that some of the words in this book might make a change. I am not suggesting in the slightest that the following is exclusively autistic, but it might be that as an autistic adult you can resonate with some of these:

- **The ability to see the world from an incredible perspective**. So many of you have so much to give the rest of the world with your incredible ability to understand the world, and all within it, from a differing perspective. Your way of processing information might be a valuable contribution – indeed, it is without any doubt at all that I can confidently suggest that many of the developments over history within various strands of science, art, nature, technology (among many others) have been the result of autistic thinking.
- **The desire for justice**. Not always, but so often within the autistic life there is a discernible element of a fervent desire for justice and 'rightness'. Many of you may even have got into trouble protecting what you feel should be protected, even though it might be detrimental to you.
- **The ability to find pleasure in perceived childish activity**. I have a real issue with the concept of how one should find pleasure – and the notion that being 'childish' or 'childlike' is somehow a negative is beyond me. Many of you have such

a refreshing and pure way of experiencing pleasure, I suspect much could be learned from your way of being.

- **Dedication and purpose.** Some of you have a staggering level of dedication and purpose, way beyond what you might find in most people. I have known people to spend years never giving up, however unlikely it might be that they will achieve their goal. Awesome.

- **Refreshing levels of honesty.** Some people might regard you as blunt, or lacking a filter – another way of understanding you is to realize that you are simply an incredibly honest person. I do sometimes wonder how different the world would be if everyone were to have the same level of honesty that is so often found in you.

- **Resilience in the face of adversity.** You are so resilient – while I might wish that you didn't need to be, it must be acknowledged that at present you may exist in a world in which you have to be resilient in order to survive, and you deserve recognition for doing so.

- **Sense of humour.** The myth that autistic people lack a sense of humour bewilders me – I can only think that whoever decided this was the case really didn't know many of you. I find that your sense of humour is sometimes incredibly clever, brings a new sense of understanding of the world, and should be guarded as extremely precious.

- **Thirst for knowledge.** I love the eagerness that some of you will show in 'finding things out' – it might not be for any gain whatsoever, aside from the joy of learning something new, an admirable characteristic indeed.

- **The ability to find joy which others might miss.** You are incredible at finding pure joy in the detail of nature, in the curvature of a spiral staircase, at the sound of a goose stepping on fresh snow – and so on, and so on. Your abilities should never be underestimated, by you or anyone else.

Last words: from a purely selfish perspective, thank you for being you. My life would be immeasurably worse off if it wasn't for you. You have taught me so much, and, I hope, made me a better person as a result. You are awesome. Love yourself.

Appendix

List of potential reasonable adjustments

Throughout the book I have come up with possible adjustments that I feel are important enough to be seriously considered by anyone involved in the autism field. I would dearly love each and every one of them to be used as examples of good practice within The Equality Duty guidelines and/or The Autism Act – whether my vision is ever realized remains to be seen! However, for ease of access, here they are in order of appearance within the book – feel free to spread the word!

1 When someone discloses their autism to you, respond by asking what autism means to them as an individual, rather than making any assumptions based on the autism label itself.
2 When you are engaging with an autistic person, always ask yourself the question, 'Am I doing everything reasonable in my power to identify anxiety and subsequently doing everything I can to reduce or eliminate it?'
3 Everyone involved in the support of an autistic person is fully aware that, at best, only *some* autism theory explains *some* of the lived autistic experiences *some* of the time for *some* autistic people.
4 It is recognized that the more anxious a person is, the more disadvantaged they are and the more likely it is that a reasonable adjustment is required.
5 If an autistic person is suffering from an emotional crash (often referred to as a meltdown) always consider using the term 'distressed' behaviour rather than the more common terms such as 'challenging' or even 'aggressive' or 'violent'.
6 When an autistic person tells you how they experience a sensory environment, make every attempt to believe them and take it seriously, irrespective as to whether you share that experience or not.

7 Autistic people are not seen within the context of being lesser; in other words, they were accepted for who they are and their natural way of being, as opposed to some kind of deficit-riddled human that is in need of fixing.
8 There is an understanding that in principle, the more options there are available to the autistic individual to meet any given requirement, the less chance there is of discrimination.
9 Never assume that the needs of any two autistic adults are automatically the same.

Further reading

Some of my previous writing, and that of others, could prove helpful:

1 Autistic anxiety
Chapter Two, *Autism and Asperger Syndrome in Adults* (2017)

2 Experiencing anxiety
'Autism and Loveliness Are Not Mutually Exclusive' in my blog: Luke Beardon Perspectives on Autism

3 Sensory issues
Chapter Six, *Autism and Asperger Syndrome in Adults* (2017)
Chapter Four, *Autism and Asperger Syndrome in Children* (2019)
Chapter Seven, *Avoiding Anxiety in Autistic Children* (2020)

4 Access to GP/hospital/dentist/healthcare
For additional reading and acknowledging the work of 'The Autistic Doctor' and colleagues see, for example, https://www.medrxiv.org/content/10.1101/2020.04.01.20050336v2

Index